Spectrology of Authoritarian Neoliberalism

Critical South

The publication of this series is supported by the International Consortium of Critical Theory Programs funded by the Andrew W. Mellon Foundation.

Series editors: Natalia Brizuela, Victoria J. Collis-Buthelezi and Leticia Sabsay

Mário Pinto de Andrade, *The Revolution Will be a Poetic Act*
Leonor Arfuch, *Memory and Autobiography*
Hélé Béji, *We, the Decolonized*
Maurits van Bever Donker, *Texturing Difference*
Paula Biglieri and Luciana Cadahia, *Seven Essays on Populism*
Antônio Bispo dos Santos, *The Earth Gives, the Earth Wants*
Sueli Carneiro, *Dispositif of Raciality*
Gisela Catanzaro, *Spectrology of Authoritarian Neoliberalism*
Aimé Césaire, *Resolutely Black*
Aimé Césaire, *Toussaint Louverture*
Victoria J. Collis-Buthelezi and Aaron Kamugisha (eds.), *The Caribbean Race Reader*
Bolívar Echeverría, *Modernity and "Whiteness"*
Diego Falconí Trávez, *From Ashes to Text*
Celso Furtado, *The Myth of Economic Development*
Eduardo Grüner, *The Haitian Revolution*
Francisco-J. Hernández Adrián, *On Tropical Grounds*
Ailton Krenak, *Ancestral Future*
Ailton Krenak, *Life is Not Useful*
Premesh Lalu, *Undoing Apartheid*
Karima Lazali, *Colonia Trauma*
María Pia López, *Not One Less*
Achille Mbembe and Felwine Sarr (eds.), *The Politics of Time*
Achille Mbembe and Felwine Sarr (eds.), *To Write the Africa World*
Valentin-Yves Mudimbe, *The Scent of the Father*
Pablo Oyarzun, *Doing Justice*
Néstor Perlongher, *Plebeian Prose*
Bento Prado Jr., *Error, Illusion, Madness*
Nelly Richard, *Eruptions of Memory*
Silvia Rivera Cusicanqui, *Ch'ixinakax utxiwa*
Suely Rolnik, *Spheres of Insurrection*
Rita Segato, *The War Against Women*
Tendayi Sithole, *The Black Register*
Maboula Soumahoro, *Black is the Journey, Africana the Name*
Fatou Sow, *Feminism in Africa*
Javad Tabatabai, *Ibn Khaldun and the Social Sciences*
Dénètem Touam Bona, *Fugitive, Where Are You Running?*

Spectrology of Authoritarian Neoliberalism

Toward a Critique of Neoliberal Ideology in Late Capitalism

Gisela Catanzaro

Translated by Pedro Hurtado Ortiz

polity

Originally published in Spanish as *Espectrología de la Derecha: Hacia una crítica de la ideología neoliberal en el capitalismo tardío*

Polity Press
65 Bridge Street
Cambridge CB2 1UR, UK

Polity Press
111 River Street
Hoboken, NJ 07030, USA

ISBN-13: 978-1-5095-6987-8 – hardback
ISBN-13: 978-1-5095-6988-5 – paperback

A catalogue record for this book is available from the British Library.

Library of Congress Control Number: 2026933118

Typeset in 10.5 on 12pt Sabon
by Fakenham Prepress Solutions, Fakenham, Norfolk NR21 8NL
Printed and bound in Great Britain by Ashford Colour Ltd

For further information on Polity, visit our website:

Contents

It is no longer possible to adopt a vantage point outside the hurly-burly that would enable us to give the horror a name; we are forced to adopt its inconsistencies as our starting point.

Theodor W. Adorno*

* "Late Capitalism or Industrial Society? The Fundamental Question of the Present Structure of Society," in *Can One Live After Auschwitz? A Philosophical Reader*, ed. Rolf Tiedemann, trans. Rodney Livingstone et al., Stanford University Press, 2003, p. 124.

Foreword

It is rare to find a book that accomplishes as much as this one does. But holding various positions together in a constellation of complexity is one of the clear strengths of this work on contemporary neoliberal authoritarianism. The geopolitical focus tends to be Argentina, but one of the main arguments here is that the regional form of authoritarianism, now consecrated by Javier Milei's enthusiastic politics of spectacular cruelty, is fundamentally related to other forms insofar as they interpret and naturalize certain givens of neoliberalism. Further, all of them must be contextualized within a radically unequal division of labor in global capitalism, but that methodological imperative can be reduced neither to a base/superstructure model nor to a monocausal explanation. Holding complexity is both a dispositive and a theoretical approach, one that demands that we rethink the very categories that have become all too settled as sites where bivalent potentials can be found: freedom, autonomy, emancipation, the nation, the people, the market, and punishment. The point is not to "reclaim" any of these in their currently constituted forms, nor to reject them as having nothing to offer to a radical critique. To treat them as "ideology" as if they were simple ideational effects and rationalizations is to misname and foreclose the potentials to be found in the field to which they belong.

For instance, for Catanzaro, "punitive neoliberalism" demonstrates that the ideology at issue is hardly "superstructural."

The contrast between ideology and discourse introduced by Foucault's barely veiled critique of Althusser in *Discipline and Punish* should not be taken as definitive.[1] Foucault objected to what he took to be Althusser's focus on state power in his account of interpellation, and formation, of subjects. While that approach traced subject formation to centralized authorities, mainly Church and State, Foucault famously insisted on decentralized operations of discourse and institutional powers as exercising productive powers and constituting the proper field of political analysis. The contrast now seems almost quaint given, for instance, the powers of the Evangelical, Apostolic, Russian Orthodox, and Catholic Churches in maintaining, building, and expanding diverse forms of authoritarian state power through both financial dealings and phantasmagoric resources of incitation.

Catanzaro proposes to rethink Foucault's *dispositifs*, once contrasted with ideology, as the way to reanimate ideology for our times. Her point is that ideology critique is not just the negative exercise of diagnosing and dismantling destructive forms of power but a way of understanding how they (a) institute themselves through subject formations and modes of naturalizing as givens the precepts of neoliberalism and (b) open each of these sites as potential scenes of opposition and transformation. Ideology critique, then, could never remain a reflexive operation of immanent thought, but rather is a mode of thinking impinged upon by historical conditions, including its enduring damage. The subject who thinks is formed through the historical conditions that constitute its object of reflection. But that reflection is not the simple reproduction of those conditions, but the site of an enduring tension where critical thought and transformative potential become possible.

Adorno is everywhere in this text, but nowhere does his understanding of the dialectic appear more persuasively than in this very notion of "tension" that Catanzaro identifies within various fields of power either ratified as "reality" or opposed through a restrictively negative version of critique. On the Left, it is all too tempting to absolutize the present, to assume that repressive powers operate as a successful totality, and to find our critical perspective within the zone of a radical outside that can only say "no" to what it finds. This form of pessimism, often associated with Adorno's strong condemnations of the culture industry, misses another potential of dialectical analysis. As the neoliberal subject is produced in contradictory ways, that is, required to take radical responsibility for itself under conditions that guarantee the failure of any such exercise of autonomy, it displays a tension between two constitutive poles of subject formation within its terms. In this way, Catanzaro brings her enhanced Althusserianism to bear upon Adorno, showing how interpellation demonstrates the very tension that can be mobilized by those seeking not only to take down neoliberalism's claim to inevitability, but also to open up a socially transformative imagination on the "ground" of that very tension.

The chapters on Argentina's politics of the last decade, including the post-Kirchner governments of Mauricio Macri (2015–19) and the current government of Javier Milei, elected in 2023, give rich detail to the vibrant and grotesque contradictions that animate the neoliberal landscape in the region. In Catanzaro's view, these two governments are not simply continuous with other neoliberal logics, nor are they continuous with one another. The specificity consists in the intensification of violence against precarious peoples, reproductive justice, and the very bodies and claims to autonomy of women, trans and *travestis*, the indigenous, and the poor. "Autonomy" here takes on an oppositional force as it counters neoliberal responsibility and the hyper-bestial powers of new manhood. What supports the establishment of neoliberalism as a "given" or a "new reality" are precisely those modes of periodization that seek to describe and naturalize this condition as an already accomplished fact rather than a scene whose internal tensions can be amplified for the purposes of both critique and social transformation. This "absolutization of the present" is accomplished through the very nomenclature that ratifies neoliberalism's conceit of inevitability: the sociological referent to "post-democracy" as if it is a true and accomplished reality; or "capitalist realism" which mocks any effort to think against or beyond its own parameters.

The problem is not just that neoliberalism becomes ratified in thought and discourse, but that its cruelty becomes both normalized and celebrated not only by the Right, but also by the now fully neoliberal political center, including portions of the center-left who resist the claims of economic justice and equality against neoliberalism. Cruelty becomes, in this book, the site where economics and phantasmagoria meet, and the meaning of "spectrology" in the title starts to make itself clear. The right-wing and fascist fascination with the spectacle of destruction – of social services, of public health, of all economic regulations against exploitation of people and land – emerges from a deep or unconscious phantasy uncovered and intensified by neoliberal advocates who seek to affirm catastrophic economic suffering as the highest expression of freedom. Like "autonomy," "freedom" becomes a term turned one way by neoliberal enthusiasts, but precisely the opposite way by those who recall Rosa Luxemburg's claim that only social freedom in the service of radical transformation should be called freedom: the freedom to dissent from government.

I am reminded of Luxemburg's remarks in *The Russian Revolution* (1918) that bear surface similarities to Macri's cries for a purifying financial freedom – freed from constraints against extractivism and pollution to mine the mountains and surrender natural resources to the potentially infinite energy demands of AI – but the differences are stark. In clarifying why freedom is the freedom to dissent, she writes, it is "[n]ot because of any fanatical concept of 'justice' but because all that is instructive, wholesome and purifying in political freedom depends on this essential characteristic, and its effectiveness vanishes when 'freedom' becomes a special privilege."[2] When freedom belongs only to the privileged, that is, freedom itself is undermined by social inequality. If Luxemburg's "freedom" is purifying and instructive, it is precisely because it would dismantle the hierarchies that both Macri and Milei affirm. That dismantling in the name of economic freedom and justice would be the new exercise of freedom, turning again, turning forward, the very discourse of purification. Indeed, a future "purified" of Milei's "pure, unrepressed capitalism" would make use of the tensions instituted by neoliberalism against its own commitments to cruelty.

The acceptance and celebration of cruelty depends upon a successful solicitation of phantasmatic content. Here Catanzaro cites Lauren Berlant's *Cruel Optimism* (2011), whose analysis of neoliberalism's cruelty foregrounds the impossibility of the phantasy upon which it relies. Those who are losing all income and all prospects are lifted by the false promise of a power to survive that, at some level, is known to be untrue. The untruth, however, only powers the phantasmatic character of the promise, converting into an intoxicated desire not only to suffer, but to cause suffering. The false promise holds out an ideal to which a nearly unbreakable popular attachment forms. That attachment to the ideal becomes more important than food or money, and those felt deprivations are converted into forms of ecstatic participation. Here "participation" is yet another site of tension to be identified and worked with, for a longing for participation is clearly one element in the scene – one that, as Gramsci might point out, belongs to no party, that is, remains available to rearticulation.

What Catanzaro takes from Berlant is the important insight into the destruction of such ideals, the remains they leave, including those whose vibrancy can be detached from the aims of destruction itself. When the images, gestures, and slogans that support the ideals of a good life, or of salvation itself, turn against those who embrace them most passionately, does the self-suffering simply amplify, or does it reveal the cracks in the ideal? Catanzaro cites Berlant, for whom a "rigid attachment to these kinds of scenes is particularly prevalent under certain historical conditions when the exigencies of flexibilization and the precarization of life produce a sense of permanent crisis – crisis as ordinary – which makes it imperative for the subject to uphold *no matter what* an appearance of continuity and normalcy."

These promises, argues Catanzaro, are not sufficient to understand the kind of cruel neoliberalism that belongs to Macri. There is a disciplinary dimension to this version of neoliberalism that is made explicit in its slogans which call for punishment, revenge, sacrifice. Self-sacrifice is but the obverse of cruelty to others, as Freudians have always known. Masochism and sadism pertain to the direction and object of the drive, not its aim. The task now is to see whether a political and historical analysis, a renewed form of ideology critique linked with a socially transformative project, can find a point of departure in such a bivalent structure. This structure is but one *dispositif* that must not only be taken apart analytically, but must be understood as one of the mechanisms that repeatedly produce subjects impinged upon, and galvanized by, such effects. As Catanzaro puts it, "the unconscious dimensions of ideology tend to go unnoticed at the level of the analysis of doctrine."

A spectral analysis is precisely one that identifies those inciting myths, legends, images, that are haunted by nostalgia and galvanized by an impossible ideal of emancipation. Under neoliberalism, that promise is indefinitely deferred at the same time, if not practically prohibited. If "emancipation" is to become a productive site of tension, a phenomenon whose bivalent structure is clearly demonstrated, the affective conditions of feeling abandoned, powerless, hateful, hopeless, will all need to be addressed and rearticulated.

That said, it should be understood that this book is an intervention in Marxism. Its final call is to overcome the pervasive and destructive division of labor at the international level, driven in part by an acute understanding of how Argentina and the surrounding regions have become the coerced handmaidens of industrial plunder from the Global North. And yet, this is also a book that lets us know that the totalizing tendencies within Marxist theory and criticism do not serve the socially transformative ideals for which radical economic and social justice movements strive. Each time a historical version of neoliberalism is totalized, the "ideological drifts" within them can no longer be discerned or mobilized for a movement of resistance and transformation. Recognizing the internal complexity and instability of an ideological formation should be the occasion for new strategy and the formulation of new ideals – or, rather, their reanimation in the service of a more equal and just organization of the world. To do so, we have to work at a "double register," that is, within a dialectical tension that never quite closes.

Catanzaro puts it this way:

> As the struggles over a new foreign debt and the struggles on behalf of workers, women, LGBTQ+, and human rights in Argentina made clear, the democratizing potential of our Latin American societies seems to lie, effectively, in *articulated* renewals of the claims for both effective autonomy and social justice, rather than in favor of one at the other's expense. In these movements, the opposition to growing economic precarity and the economization of life that makes such autonomy impossible, and the opposition to anti-intellectual tendencies that make the present absolute while pathologizing the critical impulses associated with the reflexive powers of the subject, were inseparable from the demands for social justice, which highlighted the interdependencies that sustain individual life, as well as the political responsibilities implied in the unequal distribution of a socially administered precarity.

To realize this social justice, we would have to interrupt and redirect the seduction to regard neoliberal cruelty as the order of nature and Man, one in which one suffers and inflicts suffering as the way of the world. To dismantle such a world order it will be necessary not only to contest its inevitability, but to enter its mechanisms of interpellation, the complex ways that it institutes and reinstitutes the inevitability of cruelty. The task is not only to bare its internal weaknesses and find the productive tensions it unwittingly displays, but to release the potentials found there into a rearticulation where hope and thought are no longer dismissed as foolish exercises of those who know nothing about reality. Knowing something about reality demands a critical commitment to understand how the structures of power work, how history impinges on thought and desire, how dialectical tensions are potentially productive, if not essential, to reclaiming emancipation both in and from its spectral forms.

Judith Butler
Berkeley, California, January 22, 2026

Acknowledgments

It's often remarked that every work of individual authorship is actually a kind of polyphony, not only because the voice of the writer becomes at some point indistinguishable from the theoretical traditions called upon for reflection, but also due to the collective – or transindividual – character of the work, of the uncertainties, debates, and even anxieties about the present that illuminate the writing of the text. Such a remark touches on a profound truth of this book, which cannot be dissociated from the urgent questions demanded by an ominous conjuncture whose persistence we still need to think about, and which could not have been written without the theoretical discussions that, in various working groups, we tried to organize so as to begin doing so. That is why I want to thank, first, my research colleagues at the Universidad de Buenos Aires and CONICET (National Council of Scientific and Technical Research) in Argentina, who will find in the pages ahead variations on our shared questions and our tentative answers to them. I also want to thank both institutions, which are currently resisting the threats and defunding by Milei's government, and the journals and magazines – academic and non-academic – that, despite everything, persist in the difficult work of holding space for reflection and dissonance, not only for making room for the preliminary versions of some of the ideas I present here, but above all because, with their invitations to reflect on painful, ongoing political and social phenomena, which afflict the country and the world, they in many cases collaborated with me in the development of these texts that still bear the mark of their origin as interventions. To name particular individuals now, I want to thank Leonor Arfuch, Natalia Romé, Leticia Sabsay, and Oriana Seccia for their readings and comments, Sebastián Elizalde for his collaboration in the design of the statistical content of chapter 5, Pedro Hurtado Ortiz for the translation, and Judith Butler for their generous foreword. Finally, I want to thank the publisher Cuarenta Ríos in Argentina and Polity in the United States and the United Kingdom, which continue to do the wonderful, intense work of publishing books that combine the long-lasting labor of patient reflection and the disquieting jolts produced by our recent past and present. I have had the great fortune of having woven with all of them over many years a fabric in which reflective power, political unrest, and deep friendship are inextricably tied.

Introduction

How Are We to Read Contemporary Neoliberalism?

What are the modes of critical reading that contemporary neoliberal capitalism demands of us? This question emerges from a dual suspicion about the dominant tendencies in social-historical thought that aspires to be critical. On the one hand, it would seem that, with the increasing specialization and professionalization of the humanities and social sciences, reflection about the present historical moment gradually becomes unilateral, losing the appropriate set of tensions to produce a critical interpretation of the conjuncture. On the other hand, some of the categories to which we often appeal in order to think the present seem affected by a kind of inertia, such that what was developed for a prior moment is projected onto the present, thereby diminishing our capacity to be astonished.

After the crisis of a multiculturalist utopia and of the fantasy of a friction-free capitalism, neoliberal ideology has arrived at an inflection point in which the emphasis on the unlimited potential of all individuals and their acute responsibilization, typical of entrepreneurial discourse, is combined with a new insistence on the prominent figure of punishment and self-punishment. With this new inflection, neoliberalism, first, offers an avenue for the fears and frustrations that capitalism generates, "freeing" subjects to release high levels of social aggression upon others; and, second, provides a moral codification that appeals to theological lexicons of guilt and redemption of sin in order to justify the effects of austerity politics and increasing inequality, as well as the sorrows these inflict on people's lives.

In this context, can we go on thinking of cynicism, held to be a privileged mode of 1990s postmodern subjectivity, as a useful concept to understand the present-day neoliberal interpellation? Or rather than speak of detached cynics, would it not be more appropriate to talk of embattled crusaders, ready for all kinds of sacrifices in search of a righteous recuperation of a vanquished "order"? Is it possible to continue appealing to the figures of technocracy and anti-political, pseudo-neutral management to qualify this mode of neoliberalism? Or perhaps the emergence of new right-wing movements across the world confronts us with new forms of politicization proper to a social authoritarianism whose glaring starkness would have been unimaginable a few years back? As is the case with the figures of cynical detachment and technocracy, many of the concepts developed to account for a global neoliberalism triumphant as the 20th century drew to a close – postmodern multiculturalism, depoliticization, conflict avoidance, among others – must probably be interrogated as to their analytic potency.

But alongside the question over the most fertile concepts to illuminate the outlines of the present moment comes the question over the critical modalities that the new political-ideological conjuncture demands. This is why this book takes responsibility for a certain unease regarding the timeliness of a critical model that, having shown its ability to confront the pretenses of order in previous moments, would seem at times too naïvely humanist or even rather powerless before the onslaught of efficacious rituals which are impervious to denunciations. At this level – which we might call methodological – the challenge we face is perhaps, nonetheless, the opposite of the one that emerges in the categorial realm. Where concepts are concerned, it would be questionable to indulge in that inertia which nudges thought to persist in privileging an unproblematic continuity. Yet, in the methodological realm, we could be facing the danger of making absolute the discontinuity between critical traditions and between historical periods, too readily endorsing the supposed expiration date of those styles of thinking associated with Marxism and the dialectical tradition. It would be worth asking: what do we gain and what do we presuppose when we treat as opposites the critique of a discourse's false pretenses – typically associated with ideology critique – and the poststructuralist study of rituals of productivity and *dispositifs* as if they were modalities that mutually exclude each other, devoid of immanent affinity, and among which we are sovereignly free to choose?

The critique of our contemporaneity cannot avoid marking the limits, not just theoretical but also historical, of the classic idea associated with ideology critique as the determinate negation of false pretenses of a discourse when confronted with subjective formations marked by what today is named "post-truth," or faced with discourses scarcely attempting justification or relatively indifferent to the search for argumentative coherence. Nonetheless, as one can readily witness by going back to old texts of Karl Kraus, or the work where Walter Benjamin or Theodor Adorno addressed the differences between liberalism and National Socialism, neither the doubts regarding the timeliness of inherited critical models, nor the very phenomena that sparked those doubts, are absolute novelties of our epoch. On the other hand, recognizing the risks of an implicit dogmatism in the idea that there could be a singular model of ideology critique, appropriate for all times and immune to historical change, should not necessarily lead us to affirm the expiration or sterility of critical styles that perhaps remain operative or productive in specific registers. Alongside a fetishization of novelty or the event that omits the existing continuities within the phenomena in question, an emphasis on the absolute newness of the present could well have the effect of smoothing out (or highlighting only one dimension of) ideological processes that are actually more internally complex.

In the critical interpretations of the neoliberal present collected in this book, the question over the models of reading finds inspiration in classic reflections on materialism formulated by authors such as Karl Marx, Walter Benjamin, Theodor Adorno, and Louis Althusser. As paradoxical as it may seem, to take on that philosophical-political inheritance means, nonetheless and before all else, affirming that thought is not master of its origin and must contend with the circumstances from which it speaks and which it cannot control. Unpredictable and pressing, these circumstances will not allow us to freely choose what to think, but they also alert us against that more subtle, contemporary form of subjectivism exalted in the figure of an erratic theoretical wandering. Thus, the analyses proposed here endeavor to insist on that interpretive practice known as "materialism," not so much in the sense of trying to impose an origin deemed more simply determinant or primary than others, but as a critical disposition to not abandon the theoretical and practical suspicion that theoretical-methodological questions about reading do not arise in a pure immanence of thought, but rather are always posed in relation to that which is not identical with it, something that exceeds and often hurts it, something that in a certain sense is imposed onto it and that Adorno sometimes referred to as "the force of history."[1]

As I understand it, ideology critique is constituted, in that sense, from an insurmountable tension. On the one hand, its positions are certainly not deducible from reality, from that which is given as such, and this is why the critical stance cannot avoid the gesture of transcendence with respect to that which exists, a gesture that the entire Western tradition has associated with the move to self-reflection and that poses properly theoretical dilemmas. On the other hand, the thought that has proper density or "relative autonomy" – as Louis Althusser called it[2] – never follows its own will but rather, insofar as it is a permanent interrogation of historical change, is exposed to the concrete emergence of the ideological sphere that is its object of interrogation. As Adorno suggests in the context of his reflection on the relevance and mutation of the concept of ideology – which we will examine later – this means that critiques of ideology have always been articulated and must always be articulated out of a double limit: "the theoretical construction of ideology depends no less on what actually is effectively active as ideology than it presupposes, on the other hand, a theory to define and gain insight into ideology."[3]

This paradoxical dependence on history gives rise precisely to many of the multiple transformations undergone by the now discredited concept of ideology throughout its prolonged existence as we wrestle with thinking through diverse phenomena, both concerning its context as well as the mechanisms of subjectivation and the representations of historical processes involved in each instance. To pretend that our current circumstances grant us leave from all these dilemmas and challenges represents, in fact, the opposite of a liberation, if that leads us to a solipsistic critique or an acritical isomorphism. This is why I think we need more interpreters and fewer soldiers[4] in the realm of critique too; we need more critical readers *of* – and who are stirred *by* – the complex historical tendencies acting upon us, and fewer rote wielders of consecrated theoretical frames – theoretical frames whose current practitioners will, in any event, likely abandon them as soon as academic fashion pronounces even faint skepticism about their validity. It so happens that theory does not resemble a handy toolbox at all. Theory is, on the one hand, that about which we are perennially distressed because it is never sufficient to comprehend just what is imperative to comprehend in the here and now. But it is, too, that faint possibility of illumination, that glimmer that emerges when thought turns into sparks and allows us to see – as Walter Benjamin would put it – whole zones of the past and of the present hitherto foreclosed.[5] Understood in this way, theoretical labor could never have generals or soldiers arranged in formation, but requires unsettled contenders who persist in an interpretation staunchly tethered to the real.

Written originally during the Macri dispensation in Argentina (2015–19) and spurred by events both dramatic and interpretively recalcitrant, chapters 1 to 8 attempt different approaches to the transformations of neoliberal ideology, assailed by recent crises and reconfigurations of capitalism. These texts aim to capture the intuitions and concepts that allow us to read, as closely or precisely as possible, the mutations in the sphere of subjectivity and politics.[6] In addition to the surge of a rhetoric of punishment, as well as of willing and inexorable submission, that is my focus in chapter 1 on Argentine politics during the hegemony of Macrismo, I underline two mutations at the subjective level: first, the increasing deterioration of the conditions for the production of autonomy – which coexists with an exaltation of autonomy by a discourse that is entrepreneurial, anti-intellectual, and family-oriented; and, second, a certain veering of cynicism toward cruelty, the topic of chapter 2. According to the hypothesis that has informed my reading, these features are unintelligible outside the context of increasing social precarity brought about by the implementation of neoliberal policies in the economy, and they are intertwined with a tendency to the absolutization of the present proper to neoliberal capitalism once it disdained the promise of the "globe." In turn, this absolutization seems to have spurred a totalitarian turn which does not tolerate dynamics of partiality and is suspicious of reflexivity or theoretical questioning.

Focusing on what used to be called methodological issues, chapter 3 considers the possible expiration of ideology critique in its classic formulation – a reckoning with the pretenses of a discourse in terms of the realities it produces – in the context of a tendency to increasing auto-referentiality of dominant discourses, which apparently makes them immune to questioning. To do this, I turn to the past and, taking up Adorno's reflections on the mutations in/of ideology critique imposed by the ideological particularities of National Socialism, I defend the idea of a non-harmonic coexistence of models of ideology critique found in Marx's critique of capitalism (in *Capital*). As I have already suggested, this specifically methodological level of inquiry emerges out of a double questioning. First, I ask whether the absolute dissociation of critique as either the determinate negation of a discourse's pretenses, or the analysis of the means by which subjective effects are produced, ends up stimulating an ideological drift toward humanism and moralism in the first case, and toward pragmatic functionalism in the second. Second, and this builds on the last point, I consider the possibility that the exclusive attention paid to the performativity of social *dispositifs* might in fact lead to underestimating the subjective necessity of justifications of order and social hierarchies, and to underplay the variety of ways in which that necessity is addressed, in Argentina and the world, by right-wing ideological-political discourses that endeavor to impose various kinds of moral panics. Without ceasing to work across the realm of affectivity and above all unconsciously, these discourses also produce more traditional attempts at justification – by insisting, for instance, on the beauty of a "humble yet honest life all around us," on the nobility of submissive sacrifice, and on the justice of punishment doled out to those who "didn't apply themselves and thought they could live at the expense of the State and my taxes."

Chapter 4 returns to this problematic, described by Judith Butler as a neoliberal appropriation of ethical discourse, focusing specifically on the contradictory valences accrued by subjective autonomy in the present moment across the world, and that involve a reshuffling of the politically ambivalent role played in the 20th century by the category of the individual, as it was described by Adorno in those texts where he settled accounts with moral philosophy. Constituting one of the prized monuments within that entrepreneurial ideology that, as Butler argues, renders interdependence unthinkable and makes individuals absolutely responsible for their fates, autonomy signals, also, the fragile possibility of an opening toward an interrogation of the status quo, whose future is blatantly challenged by modulations of reigning neoliberal capitalism. Celebrated as fetish, autonomy finds itself today, simultaneously, in "an era of decay," and that is precisely why its evocation turns out to be necessary for a thought committed to an emancipation still to come – a thought that will need to learn how to inflect autonomy such that it becomes unusable for discourses of self-sufficiency and an active component of a new ethics.

As for chapters 5, 6, and 7, they analyze different aspects of neoliberalism in Argentina during 2015–19 with an eye for contrasts with other countries in the region. In a way, the three chapters are haunted by the question that must be raised again and again: what is the locus, the privileged site today – if such a thing exists – of neoliberalism, and how should we refer to it? Both the interpretations of neoliberalism that are prominent in political analyses focusing exclusively on the productivity of dominant discourses, and those that conceive neoliberalism as a type of rationality whose consummation has already produced the complete subjective destitution or economization of the "I," run the risk of avoiding a question that is crucial to thinking neoliberalism's unstable social endurance. That question would be: what are the typical modes in which a subject, situated in a specific historical conjuncture with its own tradition of political struggle, manages to produce compromise solutions to deal with the injunction to entrepreneurial self-sufficiency and unlimited self-valorization? And, furthermore, how do these compromise solutions become subjectively decodable and sedimented as sensibility at a level more or less unconscious (prior to a doctrinaire attachment to a set of ideas)?

So, rather than a feat of omnipotent political engineering or a new type of rationality with inflections that remain stable across the world, I think it is appropriate to interrogate neoliberalism as a politics in Marxian terms and range it under the concept of ideology. This is to say, I aspire to interpret neoliberalism, on the one hand, in a semantic field where the present can be thought in relation to capitalism, but also in relation to a persistent yet highly imbalanced social and political conflict. On the other hand, I see neoliberalism as a complex of interpellations that project a series of impoverishing yet naturalizing alternatives – of which autonomy or social justice might be an example – that are pervasive today, and which would be the role of a theoretical-political critique to conceptualize in its specific historicity, and thus to deconstruct, instead of narrating itself using those terms.

Along these lines, in chapter 5 I reconstruct the neoliberal itinerary of the notions of justice and freedom, taking as my starting point François Dubet's and Wendy Brown's narratives of the fall of the concept of social justice. I emphasize the conservative elements in the doctrinaire neoliberalism that Brown has highlighted so as to throw light on that supposed mystery of a Right that can be libertarian and disciplinarian all at once. However, in order to understand how the new neoliberalisms can claim for themselves – and be socially perceived to be – the embodiment of a struggle *against* a putatively threatening authoritarianism and *for* the empire of order and discipline at the same time, it is not enough to study the maxims promulgated by a doctrinaire neoliberalism; what is needed is a sociological perspective able to perceive social humors, even when these are relatively disavowed by their agents. In line with this idea, and on the basis of an investigation dedicated to the political and ideological dilemmas that Argentinian democracy has faced in recent years, I propose an analysis of the predominant expectations and sensibilities in Argentine society before the arrival of Alianza Cambiemos (former President Mauricio Macri's political party) to executive office in December 2015, where we find an imbrication of deregulatory, disciplinarian, and conservative motives upon which this new right-wing formation worked, but which it did not conjure out of thin air.

Chapters 6 and 7 return to two objects that, like the question of autonomy, call for a dialectical approach: the nation and the university. To paraphrase Benjamin, on the matter of the university it would be better to inquire not so much into the opinions that institutions of higher learning hold *about* neoliberalism, but rather into all the ways in which these institutions are effectively *in* it, and vice versa – that is, to ask about the socially and politically dominant ideological tendencies that universities could problematize but that, simultaneously, affect their own internal configuration. Starting from this diagnosis,

I hold that any critical potential that the university might have *with respect to* the neoliberal present will be intrinsically related to the development of a critical and reflexive account of the university's own actuality, and to the development of a social critique *of* knowledge. But this critique should not be imagined as coming entirely from the outside, given that this practice of self-interrogation has not been foreign to practices proper to free public universities, which, in Argentina, have actually raised the issue of their contribution to social democratization in terms that transcend the mere elaboration of effective techniques – a fact that ought to be remembered by a dialectical critique of universities where neoliberalism is not wall-to-wall.

As far as the nation is concerned, the central issue is to examine the role that appeals to the national play in the dystopian, deregulatory, disciplinarian, and xenophobic neoliberalisms of our time. But also to ask if it's not a symptom of critical obstinacy – rather than potency – to prevail in the liberal assumption that the nation carries a constant value in every political discourse, independently of the circumstances. According to my interpretation, and unlike other right-wing parties in the world, the "cultural revolution" promoted by Macrismo in Argentina had the peculiarity of projecting images of a disciplinarian community where punishment is not only doled out to others but must also be endured by the national community itself. According to this discourse, this was a community that, precisely *because* it had found itself at the receiving end of a deserved punishment, had once again healthily and humbly learned to exist in the natural and subordinated position appropriate to it in the world order. In that way, by partially withdrawing from disputes between nationalisms and anti-nationalisms, the avatars of Macrismo revamped a right-wing discourse capable of articulating, without too much contradiction, the discriminatory tendencies toward certain ethnic minorities – always at the ready in the oligarchic tradition; the devaluation of the concept of national sovereignty proper to the Argentine neoliberalism of the 1990s; a sacrificial logic that encourages neocolonial positions; and a substitution of historical conflict by nature.

Like the first chapter of the book, chapter 8 was initially an intervention in the conjuncture. But if the former attempted to clarify the political situation as a new Right was consolidating power in Argentina and almost elsewhere in the region, this last chapter was written shortly before the electoral defeat of the right-wing political alliance that governed the country between 2015 and 2019, and in the middle of a heated political climate in Latin America, where unexpected popular rebellions – as in Chile and Ecuador – mixed with old-fashioned coups, like the one in Bolivia that brought down the democratically elected government of Evo Morales. The question then was less that of Ezequiel Martínez Estrada in *¿Qué es esto?* (What Is This?),[7] and more one about the marks left in the social fabric by Macrismo, and, above all, the often underestimated ideological continuities that survive through electoral periods. When it comes to imagining social powers and the limits of the future, that kind of inquiry into the vitality of specters and sensibilities of the Right becomes as urgent as the careful reading of emancipatory impulses and memories. These struggles between persistent sensibilities, bodies, and specters remind us that neoliberalism, even when it is the dominant reason, is also effect and unreason. These struggles remind us that it is something that has come to be, the unstable result of a given state of the world, and that one ought to think twice before awarding it the status of rationality.

Finally, for the English translation of this book, after four years of its publication in Spanish, I have incorporated one additional chapter about a new avatar of Argentine politics that currently seems to attract the whole world's attention: the emergence of the "Milei experiment." Following the victory of Javier Milei's ticket in the last presidential elections of 2023, it became important, on the one hand, to try to think through the subjective preconditions of that triumph, and, on the other hand, to start a discussion about its characteristics. Beginning from the presupposition that Milei took advantage of the crisis of neoliberalism that was sharpened by the COVID-19 pandemic, and proposed a strategy to manage it, I argue that he was able to tap into an experience that subjects had of leading damaged lives, and did this by subjectifying the causes of social ills, fanning the destructive energies of his audience, and channeling them in a paranoid direction in search of scapegoats – following the punitive-sacrificial strategy previously employed by Macrismo. On the other hand, the success of Milei's interpellation also depended on his capacity to bring back into play certain words that progressive forces were once known to brandish – revolution, privileges, capitalism – as well as certain images – for instance, "unrepressed capitalism" – which many people understood as more than a call for vengeance, as a sort of promise (utopia?) that far exceeded the naturalized presentism or reactionary disciplinarianism in which the rest of the country's major political forces were still trapped. Moreover, and in contrast with other avatars of the extreme, populist, or radical Right in the so-called "global North," I posit that Mileism embodies a radical anti-statism and anti-nationalism – which follows a long tradition of neocolonial submission upheld by a homegrown (neo)liberalism. Thus, it is problematic – and even Eurocentric – to identify authoritarianism with nationalism plain and simple, an identification that not only does not thematize the asymmetrical thematization of the nation across latitudes but also would seem to promote an identification of the anti-national with democracy that is very misleading in the context of recent Argentine and regional history.

1

Neoliberalism's Inflections and the Triumph of the Punitive Imagination

From "the Cultural Turn" to "Authoritarian Turns"

During the 1990s and appealing to the notion of a "cultural turn," Fredric Jameson named the specific ideology of an epoch where the unprecedented universalization of a single mode of production on a world scale was somehow celebrated as a euphoric explosion of cultural diversity in a "globe" now figured as the new and unrestricted space for the harmonious coexistence of differences.[1] With a similar emphasis, Slavoj Žižek interpreted the idea of a "friction-free capitalism" formulated by Bill Gates and the *multicultural* representation that this same capitalism produced of itself as utopias which fantasized about the possibility of becoming free not only from "the reality of material obstacles which sustain any exchange process, but, above all, [from] the Real of traumatic social antagonisms, power relations, and so forth which brand the space of social exchange with a pathological twist."[2] From a perspective closer to Foucault, around these same years, Wendy Brown saw neoliberalism as marked both by a commodified morality that exaggerated the unlimited character of a subject in a perpetual process of self-valuation, and by the diffusion of a political rhetoric that presented itself as part of a "constructivist" project where the commodification of life emerged as a horizon to be achieved rather than something guaranteed or a fact of existence.[3]

In the two decades since these statements were made and without significant structural transformations in the economic field at a world scale, many of the features of these accounts have become practically unrecognizable. Far from those optimistic and forward-looking emphases, the present state of capitalist societies seems increasingly closed in on itself. At a time where the multicultural pretense is definitively substituted by a worrisome increase in xenophobia and an explicit warmongering, the appeal to diversity and "no borders" tends to revert back to a renewed valorization of an "authentic" domesticity that would make room for the individual's true vital interests, which are supposedly "more primary" than what is postulated as artificial mediations. In light of those contrasts, even when, in the terms of ideology critique, it doesn't seem quite right to stop using the term "neo*liberalism*" to describe certain qualities of post-Fordist, unregulated, and global capitalism, it is likewise inappropriate to omit the global transformations of a system that, after the crises of 2001 and 2008, was revamped but not without having altered some of its most notorious attributes on an ideological-political level.

Thus, the emergence of political movements such as the ones represented by Donald Trump in the United States, Marine Le Pen in France, and Jair Bolsonaro in Brazil – to mention but a few, among which we would need to include the military coups in Paraguay and Bolivia – has come to cause a sort of "malaise in the nomenclature" which has as symptom the proliferation *of* and simultaneous dissatisfaction *with* the categories invoked to name those political movements. "Neopopulisms," "neofascisms," "post-democracies," or "dictatorships" – among others – would seem to say too much or too little about the configurations and strategies of the new right-wing formations at a world scale, whose conceptualization matters gravely not only for a socially responsive theory but also for any political practice oriented toward its transformation.

There is above all something in the specifically political order of the contemporary world that seems to resist conceptualization. The exclusive emphases on the association of neoliberalism and its generalized "market rationality" with "political disaffection" risk leaving in the shadows or simply unexplained the various politicizations and founding of new parties that have marked recent years. But, at the same time, the confident appeal to those traditional terms in our political vocabulary – liberalism, fascism, or populism – runs the risk of abstracting too much, by attempting to subsume what is current and actual under what has already been thought.

In tune with this categorial malaise afflicting the world, after the 2017 legislative elections in Argentina secured an impressive victory for then-President Mauricio Macri, a debate was reignited about the proper characterization of Macrismo as a political force.[4] Schematizing a little the different positions in this debate, one might say that what was at stake was whether the political phenomenon that Macri represented should be interpreted by placing the emphasis on the novelty of the emergence of a "democratic" Right in the country, or whether, on the contrary, that supposed democratic novelty could and should be interpreted as the image this political force wanted to project but was, in fact, far from real. In the case of this second interpretation, it was argued, a critical perspective ought to take some distance from that projection instead of taking it at face value, since this would risk losing sight of the very real continuities between the policies of Macri's government (2015–19) with the neoliberalism promoted by President Carlos Menem (1989–99) throughout the 1990s, or by Minister of Economy José A. Martínez de Hoz during the last civil–military dictatorship (1976–83).[5]

The perspective introduced by this second stance was particularly relevant in a moment when a certain kind of analysis of the "political game" ran amok: an analysis enamored by its objects of study and which risked reducing politics to a problem of absolute demiurges, whose alchemy could be serenely, professionally, and even-handedly evaluated according to how efficaciously it builds a "political construction" and independently of the content of that construction. If that content disappears from the analytical horizon, any interpellation could be equally likely, not only omitting the uneven character of the social and the specific ideological determinations that affect and limit any attempt at "construction," but also ignoring the partiality of the pretense of equidistance, or "symmetry" as Étienne Balibar calls it.[6] Nonetheless, the very terms of the debate between those who emphasized "the novelty of the democratic Right" and those who warned of "the continuity of the Right" had something problematic about it; something about which it is worth reflecting on if we want to better understand the socio-political process in question, and if we want to develop a better political practice. After all, even if practice does not depend exclusively on understanding, it certainly requires the most precise reading of the conjuncture we are capable of producing.

It seems problematic, on the one hand, to speak of a "democratic" Right, evoking exclusively the manner in which this Right came to power, or the politicians' discursive style, as if in Argentine national history the very label "democracy" hadn't been the subject of intense discussion. When compared to an understanding of democracy as a tense, conflictual, and unstable *process* of democratization and de-democratization,[7] this problematic version of democracy, to which an institutional political science is only too prone, entails a reduction of the concept, and should not become common sense. To trouble that reductive common sense instead of abusing the label by attaching it to our diagnoses of the new political forces entails an interpretive exercise. But this interpretive exercise is also a political practice of resistance against restrictive definitions of democracy, which aim to leave out of its concept not only enormous evidence of institutional violence – such as the violence of the security forces during Macri's government – but also the problem of rights, the material conditions of existence, and the conflictual dimension that sustains a "democratic order" constitutively open to its own transformation.

This does not prevent us, however, from discussing whether we do not lose analytical, and thus political, capacity when, granting that it is unacceptable to concede so much in the meaning of "democracy," we proceed to characterize Macrismo as *anti-political* – in contradistinction to the conflictivity of Kirchnerism[8] – as *technocratic* – in absolute continuity with the previous neoliberalism – or as merely *discriminatory*, *stigmatizing*, and *repressive*. Emphasizing the first and last of these characteristics, some interpretations of Macrismo constructed an image of Macri's government as the architect of a plundering operation supported by "the powers that be" with a special emphasis on the deployment of physical violence. Certainly, it is not a matter of underplaying the coercive dimension of Macri's project, which became more explicit with the passing of time, reaching hitherto unimaginable levels of violence with the repressive apparatus unleashed against social protest by the end of 2018 in the city of Buenos Aires.[9] But it is worth inquiring into the interpretive frame to understand that deployment of violence. Should we understand this violence, as well as the exacerbated display of the power of the State's repressive apparatus, simply as an expression of the "anti-political" or "post-hegemonic" nature of an economic project that requires physical coercion to do its bidding? This is not at all evident, because this exceedingly instrumental interpretation of repression as the means to an end (the economy) might be getting in the way of our appreciation of the central – and not merely instrumental – role bestowed on *punishment* and its promulgation across an unlimited number of images as necessary ingredients of a "re-foundational political project" that resonates rather well with what, at a world scale, might be a new punitive inflection of neoliberal capitalism.

Punishment as Ideology

When compared with the technocratic, consumerist, and multicultural modulation that marked the last decades of the 20th century, neoliberalism's new inflection, which Macrismo represented in Argentina, reveals itself as less prone to a horizon of transcendence and, at the same time, more emotional and more authoritarian. On the one hand, neoliberal capitalism has undergone a process of absolutization, losing the internal tension toward the consummation of a global society that, according to the cold technocratic utopia of the 1990s, would be forged by the hand of technical "experts" with instruments calibrated to the strictest economic rationality. After the crises of 2001 and 2008, these horizons of futurity and the aspiration to transcendence of what currently exists have given way to the inexorable verifications of the given as absolute. This is a present closing in on itself, a new "capitalist realism,"[10] that relies on not being perceived *as* problematic, and whose symptom in the fictional domain is the movement from the "Benetton utopia" toward the incessant proliferation of post-apocalyptic films in which immensely entrepreneurial subjects develop all manner of superhuman survival skills only to come up short in the face of unbearable circumstances.

In light of a capitalism fully emancipated from an outside that could mark its limits and which also lacks internal horizons, it feels necessary to observe that the vision – as ideological as this might have been – of a future without borders has been displaced by projections of walls and police fences, which express the triumph of a securitarian and punitive regime of discipline – increasingly figured as the key to the persistent conflicts afflicting the nation from both within and without. If "openness" was the mantra of what William Davies calls the "combative neoliberalism" facing socialist regimes, a "punitive neoliberalism" – which emerges when that political alternative has been vanquished and when capitalism's wheels threaten to come off after a new international crisis – encourages and interprets the social demand to "bring order" or to "return to order" as the greatest ideals to which collective subjects can aspire, to the detriment of the liberties and rights that emerge damaged in the process.[11]

If there is something tricky about the term "anti-political" when applied to the new right-wing formations in Argentina, it is not because it lacks its "moment of truth." Given that in modern times we understand politics as a potential for conflict that goes beyond a mere continuation of war and vengeance by other means, Macrismo is indeed anti-political to the extent that its disciplinarian bent leads it to see conflict in hygienic terms – that is, as a transitory and eradicable pathology even under conditions of social exploitation – as well as when it is tempted to do without mediations and welcomes vengeance and more direct forms of violence. But the trickiness of "anti-politics" emerges when this term encourages the belief in the idea that, sooner or later, a regime structured by exclusion and repression will fall of its own weight to never return. It also emerges when the attachment to the diagnosis of a tendency to de-politicization or political disaffection makes us discard the possibility that Macrismo represents a politicization of society that channels and emboldens existing social fears and prejudices, which resonate with its call to "restore order" and thus find modes of public expression. Finally, the "anti-political" label is tricky because it seems to invite us to *not* consider the specific modes of production of meaning about the present, the future, and the past spurred by that political force. In all of these dimensions, the designation "anti-political" betrays something of what Walter Benjamin called "intellectual laziness,"[12] a laziness that curtails our lucidity to dig deeper in social terms into the kinds of politicizations – and not only de-politicizations – that are possible under this form of neoliberalism, and in what way those politicizations mobilize anxieties, insecurities, and vulnerabilities generated by contemporary capitalism. In other words, the idea of the new Argentine neoliberal Right as anti-political is misleading not only because to believe in the impossibility of its persistence is comforting, and not only because it more or less acquits a society that apparently didn't have much to do with what it "said" through government institutions, but also because it doesn't help us to think through what Macri's "cultural revolution" was offering to society.

After two international crises of neoliberal capitalism – in 2001 and 2008 – this offering, articulated in every libidinal economy at the level of the subject, was no longer, as it was in the case of Carlos Menem's government in the 1990s, the promise of integration to a multicultural global capitalism, without borders and without friction. On the one hand, the new political force that came to govern after 2015 spurred a movement not toward the "globe," but toward interiority and domesticity, an "affective turn" that, quite unlike the technocratic rationality of the "Chicago Boys" era, no longer opposed passion to reason, and did not put the stress on the rationality of abstract numbers churned out by distant experts unintelligible to their audience, but aimed to speak to each about their everyday concerns, about their families and about their feelings. Society's structural problems, inequality, poverty, the increasing inequities generated by an advanced globalization emptied out of horizons, became reduced to mere willpower, confidence, and enthusiasm of the individual – an individual with a supposedly immediate "vital interest" that would summon us "all" to the unlimited community of entrepreneurs. This marked the establishment of a pre-eminence of affects and emotions over against discourse, reasons, and arguments – a pre-eminence that more or less publicly excluded certain subjects – "intellectuals" – and public institutions – universities – but that was grounded on the basic presupposition that the "interest of each" was transparent and that there was something superfluous about any individual or collective reflection about the state of the world and the needs, desires, and interests of individuals invariably trapped in it.

On the other hand, however, while it purported to cynically establish "being close" as the key to the resolution of conflicts, since its electoral victory in 2015 Macrismo proliferated in images of borders and fences teeming with security forces whose helmets, shields, and weapons in perfect alignment suggested that punitivism, not merely repressive but *ideologically productive*, would be a key ingredient in the new emotional neoliberalism. Briefly, these images ushered in the sense that we would be not only punished but also allowed to expiate a sinful past against which it was necessary to act without indulgence; they announced that we had been guilty, but that we would be welcomed in the community of punishers, which is what we ultimately *are*. These images offered, in sum, the idea of a world to which we could belong to purge ourselves of sin, but above all to make others repent for sins committed.

The Community of Punishment

The punitive features of Macrismo cannot be identified simply with an instrumental or merely exterior function because they also produce – and interpret – subjectivity. These features are neither an anomaly or *rara avis* of the contemporary "neoliberal spirit," nor are they a straightforward continuation of a previous neoliberalism. As William Davies suggests in the periodization he proposes to analyze important governmental interventions in Europe during the last four decades, despite significant continuities in the political economy, neoliberalism's identity has changed. In Davies's terms, there was a shift from the era when neoliberalism had to present itself as a worthy alternative to socialism – constituting itself as a "combative neoliberalism" from 1979 to 1989 – to that golden, or "normative," age of multicultural globalization (1989–2008), to the present "punitive" configuration, begun in 2008 and significantly marked by the unleashing of hatred and violence toward members of the population at the borders of the nation-state. Punitive neoliberalism operates, Davies claims, with a valorization of punishment that is fiercely moralistic and generates an interiorization of financial morality, which in turn produces the sense that we *deserve to suffer* on account of alleged irrationalities in our past.[13] From my perspective, this periodization proposed by

Davies is important for two reasons. First, because it suggests not an unchanging essence of neoliberalism but significant discontinuities in ideological terms, which await a more careful theorization that takes into account national and regional variations. Second, because it shows that this punitivism, hardly *liberal* in the best sense of the term, is the necessary counterpart to a capitalism that could not sustain the ideological fantasy of globalization and that lacks a golden horizon to offer. It is a capitalism that we might call "post-utopian" in the sense that, at a world scale, it is completely devoid of a *telos*, as the promise to transcend the present. But it is a capitalism that, far from being post-ideological, articulates a repressive morality and threats of physical violence by way of powerful ideological interpellations to sacrifice, as well as to actively exercise control over, and dole out punishment to, others.

At the local level, and unlike the neoliberalism of the 1990s, the re-foundational neoliberal project of Macri's party, Cambiemos, found in the figure of punishment – and not in the utopia of the globe, or in the technical expertise of Chicago economists – a crucial element. Punishment, however, was central not only or principally due to its coercive function, understood as the series of repressive operations and physical violence deployed by Macri's government,[14] but as ideology. Put differently, punishment was central in the positive image that Macrismo projected of itself. Recalling Althusser's remarks on May 1968,[15] we need to insist on the ideological power of punishment even when the very real evidence of physical violence – deployed in Argentina by the State's repressive apparatus (closely linked to judicial power) – threatens to make that power invisible. This invisibilization is problematic because while physical violence destroys subjects – tendentially destroying itself in the process – ideology produces subjects: blameworthy or guilty subjects, whose will to punishment becomes insatiable, rendering the logic of guilt and punishment tendentially eternal. We would be dealing with the devastation of the possibility of a fair and happy life even when the physical devastation fails to arrive or when the tanks stop coming.

The figure of punishment was and remains central to the prophetic discourse of Cambiemos former senator Elisa Carrió, who articulates the "post-critical" tone of this new inflection in neoliberalism which claims that "the judgment day has passed" and all that is left for us to do is to expiate our guilt through well-earned torments.[16] This figure of punishment has likewise acquired more "merciful" shades – even more insidious – in the prose of the former governor of Buenos Aires province, María Eugenia Vidal. In Vidal's speech, the crucifixion is no less inexorable but, unlike Carrió, the "fragile" governor, as if with her last breath and a tender encouragement, invites us, with pastoral demeanor, to face up to it chastely and to see ourselves as sinners who ought to welcome purification.[17] Here punishment is different from what the State's repressive apparatus and judicial apparatus do: it is different from a shot in the back – such as the one that ended human rights activist Rafael Nahuel's life – or an arrest order, such as the ones issued to large numbers of political adversaries still in prison. It is also more than a frightening bark; different from the threats promulgated by mass media prophets to ensure the prophylactic disciplining of the population. Here punishment reveals its full *unifying ideological potency* because it offers each and every one of us nothing less than *participation* in a *sacrificed community* of sinners – eager to redeem themselves by expiating the guilt we incurred when we participated in a frenzied "orgiastic squandering" which (we all suspected, according to this discourse, no matter how corrupted our souls) "had to end." The former vice-president, Gabriela Michetti, insisted on this topic toward the end of 2017: according to her, we had lived in disorder for 34 years.[18] Only contrasted with that image of flaming chaos, the present could seem resplendent: an hour of "salvation," a time when we had finally been wrested from the doom to which we had been destined since the last civil–military dictatorship ended in 1983 and to which the "coven" of "populist governments" had enlisted us. We should not interpret these pronouncements as capricious outbursts, but rather as a consistent exercise in hegemonic struggle through which we were interpellated as members of a new authoritarian community that, once again, was preparing to "leave hell."

It is crucial not to lose sight of this positive two-pronged ideological function, which is politically productive: the punishment – according to the "reinvention" projected by Cambiemos – of which Argentine society was deserving united us, in its peculiar non-utopian injunction, as blameworthy and punishers at the same time. The discourse of the then-governing party attempted to generalize a logic – typical, according to

Adorno, of the authoritarian personality – that simultaneously exacerbated *both* the tendency to condemn and sanction others *and* the willingness to submit to external authority.[19] Furthermore, to those people who could see themselves as members of that community of sinners, which became harbingers of denunciation, the supposedly moral crisis we were living through would become retroactively alive and justify the call to an implacable judgment over life and to the austerity of chastity.

The dual character of the Macrista interpellation, where one's own sacrifice and the punishment of others are two sides of the same coin, was given proper expression in the idea, broadcast widely even before Macri's assent, that enduring one's economic plight without social assistance was a sign of an individual's superiority vis-à-vis others who, conversely, became condemnable and morally inferior by virtue of accepting such assistance.[20] It was also expressed in one of the topoi that, after the coming to power of Cambiemos, became a privileged discursive motif, alongside the obsessive thematization of "insecurity": the state of "corruption" and "lack of sincerity" in which practically all Argentinians had ostensibly been immersed up until 2015. If, according to this discourse, the members of the former administration were corrupt, the people who expected "to live at the expense of our taxes" – people who received social assistance or foreigners who made use of free public services, particularly education and health care – they, too, were liars and cheats. It was against them, as against various political organizations and public demonstrations that insisted on defending these last prerogatives as earned rights, that the greatest discrimination and punitive fury was unleashed. The list did not end there, however: we had *all* been corrupt and insincere insofar as we were accessories to the sin of arrogance, which led us to imagine it was possible for a large part of the population to make use of goods and services hitherto the province of a select minority, or live in a sovereign country without debt, a country able to determine its own political economy, free from the austerity demands historically concocted by the International Monetary Fund.

So it was that these narratives of a prior, generalized moral corruption to be presently exculpated served a productive disciplinary function as key components of the interpellation of paranoid, punishing subjects, who were, at once, blameworthy and submissive. At the same time that the right to punish was generalized, the sinful state of guilt became generalized, too, together with the moral codes to guide the process of self-limitation. In this new avatar of a Right that is more "neo" than "liberal," punishment not only struck the body, but also spread blame and brought to the population the irrefutable experience of a previous crisis that every re-foundational project requires. The calvary images associated with the activist Milagro Sala[21] or the former Kirchnerist vice-president Amado Boudou[22] had a pedagogical function: to showcase the force of the sword, but above all to present evidence of a supposedly infernal past. These images were just as necessary as the monopoly over the repressive state apparatus on the part of a hegemonic right-wing project that proved itself quite capable of channeling and strengthening a pre-existing social authoritarianism. This authoritarianism seems to have been lit up by the "unbearable" experience of a critical discourse that, during the previous administrations of Néstor Kirchner (2003–7) and Cristina Fernández de Kirchner (2007–15), underlined the existence of structural inequities which had to be abolished. It was a critical discourse which, perhaps momentarily, threatened to expose the improbability of individual salvation and the emptiness of voluntaristic efforts to adapt to the insatiable requirements of the currently dominant capitalism.

2
Cruel Freedom

> Shudder, radically opposed to the conventional idea of experience [*Erlebnis*], provides no particular satisfaction for the I; it bears no similarity to desire. Rather, it is a memento of the liquidation of the I, which, shaken, perceives its own limitedness and finitude. This experience [*Erfahrung*] is contrary to the weakening of the I that the culture industry manipulates. [. . .] To catch even the slightest glimpse beyond the prison that it itself is, the I requires not distraction but rather the utmost tension.
>
> Theodor W. Adorno, *Aesthetic Theory*[1]

Neoliberalism and De-Autonomy

The idea that subjective autonomy is historically conditioned constitutes the central nerve of all materialisms. As Adorno remarks in his reading of Kant's moral philosophy, in grounding subjectivity on eternal faculties that remain indifferent and immune to poverty, we have an expression of the ideological profile of Kantian idealism and its disinterest in social responsibilities or the politics involved in the emergence of an emancipated subjectivity.[2] This chapter takes as its starting point the idea that, in addition to connecting neoliberalism's advance to socioeconomic precarity, the attack on democracy and social bonds, the critique of contemporary neoliberalism should also endeavor to explain the effects that neoliberalism has had on subjective autonomy, without falling into the temptation of adopting nostalgic positions on this issue.

To speak of the precarization of autonomy or de-autonomy[3] is a step in this direction: an attempt to name what is at risk, while avoiding hypostasizing autonomy as a default condition or as something that was once achieved and that we ought to attempt to recuperate just as it was. So, starting from the idea that autonomy is not a state afforded by some eternal faculty of the subject, safe for all time and place, the diagnosis of de-autonomy proposes that the historical conditions for its emergence are threatened by a new brand of neoliberalism, which undermines even more acutely than its predecessors the reflective instances that could expose the internal conflict and tension of the dominant imperatives and subjective common sense.

This does not necessarily entail positioning the present as a catastrophe with no links to prior moments. In a certain sense, if contemporary neoliberalism does damage to the possibility of autonomy, it is precisely *because and so long as* – as a more enlightened liberalism did with the category of the individual – it exalts it, treats it as a given and not as something that politics should be responsible for bringing about. But, on the other hand, the neoliberal inflection of capitalism undermines autonomy in a particularly active and systematic way because it presents a situation that is relatively novel in at least two respects. First because, as Judith Butler, among others, has emphasized,[4] in creating a situation of generalized, though unequally distributed, uncertainty, it undermines the social infrastructures required for an autonomous organization of one's own life in the economic sphere. Second, because neoliberalism impairs autonomy since, with its tendency to "economize the subject" (Wendy Brown[5]), it obliterates the space of tension that could produce the autonomous subject. When the moral subject is exclusively and coherently interpellated as entrepreneur, Brown argues, individual autonomy understood as a capacity for self-reflection, for rational deliberation over distinct courses of action and making decisions, flattens into a mere capacity to manage life within the terms of the given, and the practice of the subject is reduced to a mere and unlimited exercise of reproductive self-investment.

Paradoxically, far from imposing itself in linear fashion, this tendency toward de-subjectifying economization manages to realize itself in contemporary neoliberalism while promising to do the opposite. Namely, the magnification of the figure of an autonomous subject, reduced to self-sufficiency and identified with the capacity of the individual to navigate obstacles on the way to prosperity, renders the constitutive interdependence of life scarcely imaginable. In the context of an increasing precarization of life on a world scale and the exponential deepening of inequalities, the appeal to autonomy has come to perform the eminently ideological function, Butler argues, of making illegible the ties that bind us to each other. With the tendential expansion of market rationality and the ideology of self-sufficiency, individual autonomy becomes increasingly dissociated from its imbrication in transindividual processes. This not only renders invisible the ongoing, unequally distributed, and socially administered process of economic precarization, but also undermines the possibility of a democratic sociability across various spheres: the reduction of the vital interest on the part of the individual to private life (an investment in family life and divestment of solidarity); the reduction of the ideas of autonomy and individual responsibility to the obligation of personalized self-sufficiency on the part of an individual deemed "guilty" of their own fate (hyper-responsibilization); and the reduction of moral and political judgment – as well as other criteria such as the value of truth, central to the production of knowledge – to a function of cost–benefit analysis according to which the other comes to be codified in terms of a real or imagined threat to one's own self-preservation (normative homogeneity in the market sense and punitivism).

The issue is that the de-autonomy promoted by neoliberal capitalism becomes more acute in the new inflections of a neoliberalism that, both at the level of public discourses with international reach and at the level of social sensibilities, articulates increasingly punitive and anti-intellectual features in a moment when inequality has reached magnitudes not seen since the beginnings of the 20th century, and yet it somehow seems impossible to imagine alternatives to capitalism. In these circumstances, there seems to be widespread hostility toward reflection that could lead to a genuinely transformative practice linked to critical thinking. As Max Horkheimer remarked on the subject of resistance to theory in a prophetic essay from 1937, critical thinking awakens

> opposition [. . .] as theorists fail to limit themselves to verification and classification by means of categories which are as neutral as possible, that is, categories which are indispensable to inherited ways of life. Among the vast majority of the ruled there is the unconscious fear that theoretical thinking might show their painfully won adaptation to reality to be perverse and unnecessary. Those who profit from the status quo entertain a general suspicion of any intellectual independence.[6]

Much like in Horkheimer's historical moment, in our contemporary punitive neoliberalism, reflection as such becomes suspicious while, as Davies suggests, language is increasingly detached from its epistemological or semiotic aspirations to represent reality and instead offers empty affirmations, or confirmation schemes, which are, on the contrary, means to reinforce reality. We could say, anticipating our later discussion, that it is thanks to these more or less subtle mechanisms, whose effects would seem foreign to all violence, that a certain violence and a certain power become constituted: namely, the ideological power of anti-intellectualism, understood as the appeal to the transparency of the world and even of our own subjective desires, opacity in general crumbling under the weight of our supposedly immediate, vital, and self-evident interests.

Valences of Anti-Intellectualism

> For me to master nature, I have to think. But by thinking, I interpose a medium between the object of action and myself that strives to go beyond both. The gesture of the savage who pauses for an instant to reflect whether or not he wishes to eat his prisoner contains teleologically the end of violence.
>
> Theodor W. Adorno, *Towards a New Manifesto*[7]

During Mauricio Macri's presidency, the emotive trends toward an anti-intellectualism that, on a world scale, are becoming increasingly visible as an intrinsic component of a punitive neoliberalism were soon expressed in a negative or repressive modality. Some of their earlier indices were pathologizing stigmatizations directed at various characters associated with "intellectual life," voiced by officials from the administration – starting with the head of it – and that were synthesized in a pseudo-vitalist diagnosis by the philosopher and presidential advisor Alejandro Rozitchner: in his view, Argentina suffered from a "critical frenzy" which it was necessary to suppress from education so kids could be "happy, capable and productive."[8]

But even as it made room for this exercise of stigmatizing identification and even openly censured certain individuals, the anti-intellectualism promoted by Macrismo did not stop at the witch hunt of "intellectuals"; it was also made manifest in the harassment of institutions of higher education by members of the government and by the dominant media outlets. Even though, as usual, it primarily inveighed against the free and public national universities, this harassment also strengthened the typical privatizing discourse of neoliberalism, sowing doubts about whether it was even worthwhile attending college, claiming that it was irrelevant in today's world, and pontificating about more "flexible alternatives" such as those provided by "vocational and technical education."[9]

Both the discrediting of universities and the pathologizing stigmatization of certain individuals associated with critical reflection highlight the repressive resonances of anti-intellectualism as an interpellation that invites subjects to identify, condemn, and punish others. Nonetheless, the visibility of this repressive profile, whose manifest violence tends to capture critical attention, should not pull focus from another dimension, more insidious, in which anti-intellectualism is experienced by the subject, not in its negative inflection as stigma and condemnation, but in its "positive" inflection as a release – an emancipation from alleged "convoluted" and "fallacious" arguments that insisted on lingering too much on the past and furthermore undermined one's own singularity. At this level – which in Argentina became entrenched by the vague social intuition that during the "populist governments" the "authentic" and "natural" desires of the population had been hidden by a thorough ideological polarization of social life – "anti-intellectualism" is not properly a consciously held idea about the undesirability of universities or the so-called "intellectuals," but rather the feeling of despondency experienced by someone who is told their "true concerns" are affected by abstract and distant issues, when in fact reality – this discourse claims – is much simpler than all that: one already knows what one wants.

Underlying all the evidence of physical violence or direct persecution, anti-intellectualism is here a more or less seething suspicion, more or less unconscious, against everything which in our collective experience – and not only in that of so-called "intellectuals" – cannot be satisfied with what is already known and, because unsatisfied, has to ask again, hoping to recover lost or difficult-to-imagine pieces of the puzzle. Its insidiousness in democratic life lies in the fact that when fantasizing about a world fundamentally transparent and a subjective desire equally transparent to itself, anti-intellectualism not only designates easy targets to bear the ire of a subject facing an increasingly uncertain world, but it also seeks to erase that which is lost in collective and individual experience when only what is given can be real. As this anti-intellectualism marches on, it joins the fetishistic exaltation of autonomy promoted by neoliberal entrepreneurialism – which, of course, turns a blind eye to its material conditions of possibility – and the market-sanctioned harmonization of conflicts over value from which the ethical subject is supposed to emerge. All of these are added to the tally of attacks on autonomy derived from the cult of the given and of a heightened ritualization of discourse that pretends to unveil every dissonance or subjective hesitation in the face of "evidence" as a superfluous, if not outright pathological, negativity.

Now, under what conditions do we see this contorting of neoliberalism, which, in Argentina, it would be worth characterizing – following an early insight of Horacio González – as a renewed emphasis on domestic life that expels the "contingency of history"?[10] The hypothesis I wish to develop in the remainder of this chapter is that the ideological climate that Macrismo helped usher in and of which Macrismo is an expression cannot be thought of as a mere continuity with previous neoliberal logics. In fact, it demands the conceptualization of new forms of violence – violence to the possibility of the reproduction of bodies, to autonomy, and to language – that emerge alongside the becoming absolute of the present, which Fredric Jameson, among others, has hailed as one of the marks of postmodernity,[11] and has become even more acute at a world scale since the crisis of 2008. As we will see, it is this absolutization of the present, alluded to in different ways by the ideas of "capitalist realism" or "post-democracy,"[12] that at both a subjective level and the level of legitimating political discourse tends to express itself in the transition from what we could call the old multicultural cynicism to contemporary cruelty.

From Cynicism to Cruelty

Cynicism was one of the features of neoliberal subjectivity most insisted upon by critical thought at the turn of the 1990s. In *The Sublime Object of Ideology*, rehearsing Peter Sloterdijk's formula, Slavoj Žižek insisted on its illusory character:[13] cynicism was the illusion of being beyond the illusion. But he also emphasized that it was an *enlightened* false consciousness, which pretended to situate itself beyond all universalist ingenuity and declared openly its own particular interest. The typical gesture of the cynic was disdain in the face of universal pretenses, understood by the cynic as plain impostures. The cynic didn't search for a less damaging universality, but they sought to "bleach" the despised particularistic ground, which, "ultimately" – they declared in a knowing tone – constitutes the only real substrate of all practice. Cynicism, as public conduct – María Pía López wrote in sympathy with Žižek – makes a gesture of skepticism and profits from it for individual gain: "If everything is lost, I'm here to grab what is left [. . .] and I have no qualms about saying it."[14]

It is indeed tempting to think of the regime of post-truth – which many authors claim is currently expanding – in terms of the obscure game the cynic plays with truth. However, it is worth asking whether by collapsing the two we are skipping over some key questions about a present moment that tends toward conventional values rather than skeptical ones, and that, as we saw in the previous chapter, seems more in thrall to the logic of punishment and sacrifice than to unabashedly avowed egoism. No doubt, the difference between expressions of cynical incredulity and absolute, militant certainty cannot be thought in terms of a simple opposition between unbelief and belief, not only because – as Žižek insists on – the cynic holds tight to the illusion of being beyond illusion, but also because both sides of this opposition agree on confirming what is and converge on the recognition that only what is given is possible.

But if in both cases what ends up being confirmed is actually the ineluctability of this world that produces suffering, for the cynic – who remains steadfast in their conviction that they will be saved despite what others think – suffering is not yet an inescapable fate with no outside. That absolute fate is only consolidated as inescapable when the idea of salvation inside or outside the system is foreclosed. When promises of transcendence – even within the neoliberal capitalist order – come tumbling down, as they did at the level of social imaginaries after 9/11 and then with the financial crisis of 2008, what becomes absolutized is not only the present as such but also an awareness of the ineluctability of suffering – at this point, then, cynicism tends to evolve into cruelty.

According to Lauren Berlant, from the perspective of the individual psyche, "cruel" is the rigid attachment to a fantasy scene independently of its content and the possibility of satisfying the promise associated with it. What is cruel about these attachments and not just inconvenient or tragic, Berlant says, is that the subjects

> might not well endure the loss of their object/scene of desire, even though its presence threatens their well-being, because whatever the *content* of the attachment is, the continuity of its form provides something of the continuity of the subject's sense of what it means to keep on living and to look forward to being in the world. [. . .] if the cruelty of an attachment *is* experienced by someone/some group, even in a subtle fashion, the fear is that the loss of the promising object/scene will defeat the capacity to have any hope about anything.[15]

Berlant is interested in thinking about what happens when the objects or scenes that sustained those idealized images of the good life are in tatters or shattered, and when, in increasingly dire conditions of economic and affective precarity, adjusting comes to seem an achievement. Their hypothesis is recognizable as a politicization of the Freudian picture. On the one hand, Berlant argues that since people don't tend to gladly abandon a libidinal attachment, they persist in that attachment even when the possibility of its realization is close to nil, and even when persisting in those idealizations is actively undermining that very possibility. But, on the other hand, Berlant also argues that a rigid attachment to these kinds of scenes is particularly prevalent under certain historical conditions, when the exigencies of flexibilization and the precarization of life produce a sense of permanent crisis – crisis as ordinary – which makes it imperative for the subject to uphold *no matter what* an appearance of continuity and normalcy.

Corresponding to these historical conditions in the aesthetic realm, Berlant claims, is a new genre whose specificity they delineate in a comparison with the situation comedy, and that could be useful to consider in order to think through the difference proposed earlier between, on the one hand, a neoliberalism that is particularist yet multicultural, global, and cynical, and, on the other hand, a new neoliberalism without a utopia of reconciliation, at once more conventional and cruel. If in sitcoms, personality is figured as a limited set of repetitions that will inevitably appear in new situations, what makes them comic and not tragic is that, in the genre's imaginary, the world holds for us a kind of place that allows for our enduring existence. By contrast, the protagonists of the situation tragedy oscillate between having something and being ejected from the social, which makes them try, against all odds, to sustain normative scenes of intimacy and a family that might bring a sense of normalcy – without the possibility of respite in the face of a constant struggle for survival and the demands of self-valuation, reproducing therefore the kinds of non-reciprocal relationships that are constitutive of the permanent state of crisis in which they are immersed.

Keeping in mind Berlant's allusion to the possibility (or impossibility) of subjectively experiencing the world as a place that allows for our survival and taking up our previous counterpoint between cynicism and cruelty, we could say that the cynical indifference to the promises of universal reconciliation was only possible in a time that – as torturous as this was – persisted in upholding those promises *and* the subjective game of disaffection. After the image of a multicultural Globe was traumatically exposed as illusory, and as the image of a friction-free capitalism came into crisis, the promise of neoliberal capitalism, particularly in regions most affected by precarity, seems to consist mostly in the end of promises, or rather in the paranoid affirmation of a hierarchical, unequal order as the only possible promise.

So, while cynicism was the exacerbation of a particular interest that had no qualms about insisting on its own interested particularity, the new neoliberal discourse, by contrast, threatens to disinvest completely from the logic of interest and self-preservation, summoning us to an *unlimited* sacrifice, and openly declaring that we will suffer. According to this message, which was made more or less explicit by several representatives of Macri's government, we would do this not in search of a lost supremacy – akin to the slogan "Make America Great Again" – nor with the purpose of reconquering it, but because we will have recovered our senses, an awareness about the proper place reserved for each country and each individual in the "normal" order of the world[16] and the social hierarchies therein. This is why what is recuperated is, from the perspective of this discourse, nothing but the sense of "justice in inequality," the inequality of an order whose re-establishment promised – even when it didn't seem to promise anything else[17] – to soothe anxieties related to a social structure whose hierarchy was believed to be in flux.

This disciplinarian aspect of contemporary neoliberalism is made explicit in the motifs "insecurity" and "corruption," privileged focal points of the cruel social justifications where (self-) sacrifice and the punishment of others emerge as two sides of the same coin. These narratives present sacrifice not as something simply circumstantial, but as inherent to our nature, good, and even "freeing," in the sense that assenting to its necessity releases us of false expectations and partially absolves us of the sin of pride in having had those expectations, by teaching us to stay in our proper place and, above all, granting us the right to teach others – whether those victims of the "tall tale of social justice" or the appropriators of a right "they didn't earn" – to occupy their subordinated place in the order of things, even when this implies a threat of direct violence. In this disciplinarian sense, insecurity and corruption are the scourge that threatens the social body and which need to be expunged from that body no matter what; the motifs of insecurity and corruption offer those submissive subjects, in thrall to the unlimited and unsatisfiable demands of self-sufficiency, the opportunity to imagine a semblance of stability in "evil" and – counterintuitively – in themselves in the midst of a constant state of exception produced by contemporary capitalism. By contrast, abandoning that fantasy of order under conditions of permanent extraordinariness could mean for them, as Berlant suggests, a precipitous fall into a state of non-belief, a state where it is no longer possible to believe in anything at all.

However, if these (self-)punitive narratives turn out to be paradoxically associated with the subjective expectation of reclaiming freedom, above all this is the case because one finds that these narratives offer something more than a stable, disciplinarian representation of the self and of others within a hierarchical, fixed order. With these narratives, one does not only free oneself from a "chaotic," "anarchic" world where one's "own place and effort is no longer respected," but above all one becomes imaginatively free of one's own impotence to represent the world, by imagining oneself capable of clearly tracing the coordinates of an incomprehensible reality so resistant to examination. The opposite of the experience of impotence is the earned certainty of someone "who already knows everything they need to" – as the former president Macri put it in the interview with *Perfil* cited earlier – and it is actually that fantasy of representational self-sufficiency that seems to free them – even more than discipline – from the experience of vulnerability.

To remain conveniently attached to the shifting conventional discourses that an enlarged culture industry regularly puts on offer as a way to map differences and administer guilt and punishment as needed constitutes an essential feature of the subject's psychic economy, one that leaves no room for doubt. Not even the cynical doubt that in the 1990s in Argentina looked suspiciously at the heteronomous character of the themes and values that with each passing day entered and exited the "agenda." Unlike that cynical subject who didn't believe in anything, "not even in what you hear on TV," the cruel subject interpellated by Macrismo had to hold on fast to those discourses. Conceived as a currently expanding tonality in the general affect of our time, cruelty is nihilistic, but not so much in the sense of a sly cynical suspicion of universals and values. As Wendy Brown has suggested,[18] this nihilism consists rather in the becoming banal of those values with respect to which the subject holds an attitude that – appealing to Adorno's conceptualization of conventionalism in the 1940s – we could describe as simultaneously rigid and absolutely flexible: rigorist *and* docile to prevailing opinion.[19] The inflexible cruelty which characterizes this epoch could be read, in that sense and paradoxically, as a symptom of the complete over-adaptation demanded by a fundamentalist capitalism in which logics of partiality and particularities – egoistic or not – will have to be displaced by a logic of the absolute.

3
Is the Critique of Ideology Obsolete?

In the text about the concept of ideology already mentioned in the introduction, Adorno situated the question of critique around the relation between ideology and the bourgeois spirit. Ideology, he says, is justification. "It presupposes the experience of a societal condition which has already become problematic and therefore requires a defense just as much as does the idea of justice itself, which would not exist without such necessity for apologetics."[1] It is around this problematic/apologetic substratum of the liberal bourgeoisie that ideology critique, understood as "confrontation of ideology with its intimate truth," or as determinate negation, "confrontation of ideal entities with their realization," can do its work. But, Adorno says, if one wanted to critique along these lines the so-called "ideology" of National Socialism, one would find oneself the

> victim of an impotent naïveté. [...] The critique of totalitarian ideologies has not as its task to refute them, for they make no claim to autonomy or consistency at all, or only in the most transparent fashion. What is indicated in this case is rather to analyze on what human dispositions they are speculating, and what they wish to evoke from these – and that is hellishly far removed from such official declamations.[2]

Here we have two opposing models of ideology critique, urged by, respectively, bourgeois liberalism and National Socialism.[3]

The first model belongs to the tradition of false consciousness critique deployed as the reading of symptoms, attending to what discourses must omit – whether external reality or its own discursive lapses – to conquer coherence (or unity) and uphold the acceptability of the current order. In the second model, however, consciousness itself is one of the subjective effects that come to be formed above all in the realm of drives – indifferent to standards of coherence or truth – via rituals that the critic must not try to refute or expose as contradictory but rather analyze insofar as they are productive.

Adorno's argument points to the fact that we cannot choose one of these models starting from purely theoretical considerations. On the contrary, he reminds us of the objective qualities of the ideology in question as a determining element in our choice of methodologies. These, much like their objects, would seem to emerge linearly one after the other, were it not for his fleeting remark where he troubles the certainty that, even under an authoritarian regime, it would be possible to *absolutely* do without justifications. That anxiety becomes interesting because, even though it refers back to a different historical situation, it would seem to return to a tension that is present also in Marx, whose critique of capitalism does not always operate on the same level, nor does it advance harmoniously by evoking always the same terms.

Marxian *Mythologiques*

In effect, Marx mobilizes different modes of ideology critique, even in the same book, *Capital*, whose most-read chapters, I and XXIV – devoted respectively to commodity fetishism and primitive accumulation[4] – could be considered paradigmatic examples of the two critical models alluded to by Adorno. Chapter XXIV is a refutation of the self-understanding of capitalism as the overcoming of barbarism, and its indelible impact over generations is linked to the moral commotion it evokes in the reader.

What liberalism remembers as a peaceful, dignified history of intrepid gentlemen is revealed by the critic as a consistent larceny in the course of which "noble men" exercised all kinds of iniquities to turn entire generations of men and women into an amorphous mass of dispossessed peoples toward whom we cannot but feel empathy. Marx not only does not renounce this feeling of empathy but also invites the reader's outrage, rattling our senses to contemplate the enormity of the wrong addressed to the men and women of the past. But few things could be more out of sync with this moral commotion than the careful, almost jovial, disposition that he simultaneously demands in his readers as he unravels the "secret of commodities" in chapter I, where critical knowledge of the present would seem to demand sagacious detectives rather than outraged humanists.

If in the first model of ideology critique – that is, the one that comes second in *Capital* – the reader is addressed as a peer and witness to the false pretenses of social pacification upheld by the dominant class, in chapter I, they are addressed instead as if they were an objective analyst of an amazingly complex machinery. And if in the narrative of primitive accumulation the idea was to confront the liberal doctrine with the unavowed blood-soaked genesis of capital, here we're dealing with a dispassionate analysis of the mechanisms that produce and uphold such fictions. The first critical model is bound with a judgment over what exists and the confrontation – as Adorno would put it – of ideal entities with their realization, whereas the second model insists on knowing how what has come to be works, and, above all, how it manages to produce such powerful mental and emotional alchemies. The former confronts us with the mud and blood of history; the latter invites us to disassemble its logic.

What's peculiar is that Marx's critical model recovers them both at once, without bothering to smooth over the tension provoked by their coexistence, and, we should add, without minimizing the emerging conflicts that await the reckoning of these *epistemological* critical modes with the requirements of a different practice: *political* practice, which does not rest after denouncing the myth, or with analyzing its conditions of possibility or perdurability, but insists on the necessity of "playing the part" in the theatrical sense, that is, of *activating the myth*.

This political – rather than critical-cognitive – dimension of ideology takes center stage in *The Communist Manifesto*, but can be detected, in effect, also in chapter XXIV of *Capital*, where Marx, after insisting over several pages on the falsity of the "myth of economic original sin," does not hesitate to advance the scarcely justified claim that alongside misery revolt grows.[5] Even though we cannot dwell on this point, I cannot avoid pointing out that in the state of moral commotion that this narrative elicits from us, the claim that insurgence grows as misery does is less a serene attestation of an "ineluctable tendency" deduced scientifically – as Marx himself would like to think – than a *call* to action, an exhortation to insurrection through which the narrator activates *another* myth: the myth of class struggle. With this third appearance of ideology in Marx's text, a "political excess" enters the scene, an excess that – despite the accusations of scientism – remains central to his treatment of ideology. We're dealing with an insurmountable mythical dimension that is constitutive of the revolutionary practice of Marxism as it relates to class struggle. As Althusser remarks in *On the Reproduction of Capitalism*, not only does this reference evoke a key concept in this new *science* of history, which has been enlivened by Marx's reflections, but it is also a crucial piece of the conflictual *ideology* proper to the proletariat.[6]

But going back to my main argument about the coexistence of two critical models in *Capital*, it's worth asking how we should interpret this simultaneity. What would be the relation of the second model of critique – where ideology emerges above all as ritual, objectivity, *dispositif*, mechanism, or apparatus capable of producing certain effects and configuring subjectivity – with that other, more classical and humanistic dimension of ideology critique that operates at the level of doctrine and where the harmonistic pretense of a dominant discourse unravels? Would it be right to say that one model is the overcoming of the other, which would then have the status of a theoretical wrinkle to be smoothed over in the Marxian text? This question has repercussions beyond Marx. Would it be possible to assume, for example, that the analysis of the productivity of *dispositifs* or Ideological State Apparatuses, in Althusser's term, is theoretically superior to the critique of ideology that operates at the doctrinal level as symptomatic reading of discourses and/or that deals with justifications? Would it be preferable to argue that such so-called "superiority" is in fact historically and not theoretically determined, insofar as the analysis of the mechanisms that produce subjective effects demonstrates greater sensibility and acuity with respect to ideological trends in late capitalism? Are we dealing with both things at once: a theoretical supersession that maps onto a historical one? What if we were facing differentiated analytical dimensions that don't find such absolute historical limits and actually coexist – with varying degrees of importance and weight that one would need to determine case by case – inside past ideological configurations, as well as in ideological configurations contemporary with us, and whose decipherment we have set as our task today?

Upholding Dissonance

With this reference to the present, the issue of inheriting a complex critical tradition becomes something more than a speculative exercise turning on past authors and becomes an urgent problem for us in the here and now – a problem which, for that very reason, is worth interrogating theoretically. Is it not a loss for critical thought when we postulate these two modes of critique as absolute alternatives, without possibility of articulation and/or coexistence, even in conflict and disharmony? What would be the appropriate critical attitude to uphold vis-à-vis this tension or critical incoherence today? In sum: how to deal with this dissonance, not so much as a positioning vis-à-vis the Marxian text "in general," but in particular, in the context of the present moment, one of whose features is precisely to ape the hyperinflation of rituals and the occlusion of subjective experience associated with totalitarian regimes, but that nonetheless is prolix in its production of justifications seeking to legitimate existing social hierarchies; a moment where subjects – despite the precarization of the conditions of possibility of autonomy – cannot seem to do without narratives about their own lives that allow for the production of descriptions and judgments about the existing order, as well as give meaning to their place as subjects in that order.

As Žižek has suggested,[7] and as Étienne Balibar has remarked in his criticism of Wendy Brown,[8] the ambivalence between the analysis of the tautological and performative element of ritual, on the one hand, and the interpretation of narratives that promote the desirability of the status quo, on the other, does not necessarily indicate a critical fault, but could be taken as the sign for a need to understand the ideological conjuncture in terms of conflicting tendencies, asymmetrical but not univocal, in contemporary capitalism, which would therefore call for a certain juxtaposition of theoretical paradigms and critical modulations, not unlike the juxtaposition rehearsed in the early Marxian critique of capitalism. In that sense, not abandoning ideology critique as the critique of justifications of order could be alerting us to a de-politicizing, fatalist bias in accounts of neoliberalism as a type of rationality whose de-subjectivizing logic would be actualized without encountering resistance.[9] But in general, we could say that the advantage of insisting on a tense articulation of these two critical models is twofold. On the one hand, it has a de-totalizing effect that calls our attention to the possible ideological drifts associated with the absolutization of each of these models. On the other hand, it invites us to formulate a multidimensional focus capable of attending to the inner complexity of ideology today.

As for the de-totalizing effects of the multifaceted Marxian critique, in addition to marking the limits of the enlightenment critique of false consciousness[10] by mobilizing two models of ideology critique simultaneously and without minimizing the friction between them, Marx allows us to observe their respective limits, not letting the classic critique of ideology descend into moral condemnation of capitalism's effects, and not letting the analysis of ideological mechanisms become a functionalist or pragmatist drift of immanent ideological critique. The former follows a principled and humanitarian impulse that leads it to condemn violence and effective misery. From a transcendent position with respect to what currently is, this model argues that violence and misery should not exist. But as moral critique leaves unquestioned the social conditions of production of such effects, the actual conditions of inequity and the contemporary naturalization of sacrifice and punishment tend to become, for this genre of critique, a fatality that can only be repudiated through denunciation of some of its dehumanizing consequences. By contrast, the pragmatic disposition undertakes an investigation of what works and how it works. With an immanent strategy, it ideally seeks to guarantee a greater efficacy for alternatives to capitalism, whose dominating logic, nonetheless, it must recognize as determining all possible action, if not identical to logic as such. But when it does this, the pragmatic critique generally tends to turn that "logic" into the absolute horizon of all "realist" practice in such a way that, again, the current situation becomes eternalized. Only this time we are not dealing with the emerging eternalization of an immutable world vis-à-vis the contemplative moral horror of censors who have renounced asking about causes and the possibility to transform injustice, but the eternalization of the given as it emerges from a naturalized practice of the dominant modes. The persistence of a two-pronged critical model allows us, by contrast, in Marx's case, to uphold the tension between immanence and transcendence, between description of effective mechanisms and the disposition that reacts against what is given, enlivening a dissonance that avoids the self-serving collapse of the dilemmas surrounding moral action.[11]

As for the ideological dimensions of the present that this methodological irresolution would help us to conceptualize, as we have seen, contemporary neoliberalism confronts us with an exacerbation of the ritualistic dimension – theorized by Marx as it concerns the fetishism of commodities or by Althusser in his theory of Ideological Status Apparatuses[12] – that produces forms of empty affirmation quite similar to those described by Adorno in his account of National Socialism, and whose efficacy lies in confirming the given by mere repetition. Clearly, such systems of confirmation, which characterize a large part of new right-wing movements, cannot be deactivated via simple confrontation of those discourses with reality, or with their own omissions and internal incoherences. For a critical perspective, the challenge would rather be to theorize the mechanisms and modalities by which they "take hold," as Althusser would put it, at an unconscious level.[13]

But, on the other hand, as Adorno seems to suspect even in the case of National Socialism, it is not obvious that the same orders that self-reproduce themselves in these rituals can totally do without the production of a justificatory system that would allow subjects to bestow argumentative consistency and moral validity to those statements, judging them as more or less apt to describe the world they live in.[14] In this sense, the crises that neoliberalism has gone through, first in 2001 and then in 2008, could have had a paradoxical effect. If, on the one hand, in the defensive/absolutizing gesture that we described in earlier chapters, the ritual dimension of this ideology was reinforced with the revamping of a post-crisis capitalism, on the other hand, faced with the crisis of the illusion of a multicultural, friction-free capitalism, there emerged also a political need to reinforce the dimension that Adorno called apologetic, and that we described when referring to the promise of liberation and justice contained in the discourse of sacrifice and expiatory punishment in Argentina's public sphere. Likewise, in other contexts, conditions of extreme precarity hitherto quite plainly denied had to be, as a result of the crisis, discursively incorporated and justified – for instance in meritocratic terms – precisely so the dominant ideology could configure itself as "lived experience" in the Althusserian sense: that is, in the sense of an illusory *allusion* to reality that allows the subject to assume as non-problematic and self-evident certain presuppositions, such as the structural character of scarcity and the impossibility of overcoming inequality. Could the critique of ideologies, then, avoid confronting, as Adorno would say, the order's pretenses with those other realities that such an order produces to guarantee its reproduction? If we were to dismiss as archaic the critique of ideology as negative determination, would it not undermine the possibility – already extremely fragile – of pointing out existing discrepancies between, for example, the pro-dialogue declarations of the new Rights (such as Macrismo) and the simultaneous increase in repression exercised by their governments; between the proclamations of higher quality of life and widespread social precarization; between the affirmation of self-sufficiency and increasing levels of dependence – individual and national – that are today a staple of many Latin American countries?

Without a doubt, we cannot forget that, as we have mentioned, justifications and narratives function to a large extent for the benefit of those who are already believers, and that such an order of belief constitutes itself massively in instances that are unknown to the subject and in light of which justifications would be better conceptualized as rationalizations. However, it would not be appropriate to collapse an ideology that is forced to harbor a problematic state of the world – and for that reason has to produce its apologia – and an ideology that does not. Ideologies are not all the same, and despite that fact, it is often difficult to point to differences from the perspective of ideology critique understood as the analysis of mechanisms that produce subjectivity. Conversely, the unconscious dimensions of ideology tend to go unnoticed at the level of the analysis of doctrine. All the more reason then, if that were even possible, to refuse to choose between both models. Their respective virtues become apparent precisely when they discomfort each other.

4

Paradoxes of Autonomy (and Its Critique)

Judith Butler and Theodor Adorno

> ... amid the universal unfreedom each trait of humanity wrung from it grows ambiguous.
>
> Theodor W. Adorno, "Messages in a Bottle"[1]

Minima Moralia, Again

In a text from 1965 that returned to the necessity of upholding at once a drive to understand and an intuition of the irrationality of the reigning social systems in the context of advanced capitalism, Adorno remarked on the ineluctably dual character that the category of the human took on under the then-dominant historical conditions:

> If we were looking for an ideological justification of a situation in which men are little better than cogs to their own machines, we might claim without much exaggeration that present-day human beings serve as such an ideology in their own existence, for they seek of their own free will to perpetuate what is obviously a perversion of real life. So we come full circle. Men must act in order to change present petrified conditions of existence, but the latter have left their mark so deeply on people, have deprived them of so much of their life and individuation, that they scarcely seem capable of the spontaneity necessary to do so.[2]

Facing what around those same years Althusser conceptualized as the ideology of humanism, Adorno concurred in the importance of analyzing the function that the category of the human served in the context of the dominant ideology. Adorno, however, concluded that what was necessary was not to break with the humanistic problematic, but rather to develop a certain paradoxical relation with it in one's critique of society. According to him, this critique entailed successive re-encounters with the terms once associated with the promise of emancipation, which had nonetheless become key figures in the reproduction of domination and perpetuation of injustice. Such was the case with one of the centerpieces of moral philosophy: the category of the individual, which, at the very moment of its decay – he argued in *Minima Moralia* – had come to speak the truth.

The fact is that the truth of concepts and categories is marked, in Adorno's reflections, by a "temporal index" – systematically ignored by the liberal tradition, as well as by neo-ontological projects like Heidegger's – that it is the task of critical thinking to elucidate. Therefore, far from taking the category of the individual as a primary category, empirically evident and valid for all time – as is the case for a political liberalism – for the immanent critique of liberalism that Adorno pursues in *Minima Moralia*, this category might contain a critical potential *in the period of its decay*, contributing to an understanding – of the problematic status of individual experience and the nullity of the individual under capitalism – that the very term individual "had merely obscured" when it stood as a dominant concept.[3]

But if it was the work of the critique of society to expose the temporal index of these categories, that same index exposed critique, in turn and necessarily, to an excess of its object that precluded the possibility of fixing once and for all a critical language, capable of determining in a definitive and univocal manner the emancipatory potential of all these terms. On the one hand, in advanced capitalist societies, affirming the individual as primary and a given was nothing but ideology, because through it the social mediation of the individual fell by the wayside, and because, with the affirmation of the eternal centrality of the individual and the celebration of its splendor, the social production of nullity of concrete individuals in a mass society became opaque.[4] On the other hand, however, the critique of the false reconciliation between individual and society could not do without the category of the individual that, as the sign of what is currently dominated, constituted itself as one of the key instances in which it was possible to read the unfulfilled promise of happiness and the persistence of harm, embodied in the isolated individual as the model of all individuation: "If today the trace of humanity seems to persist only in the individual in his decline, it admonishes us to make an end of the fatality which individualizes men, only to break them completely in their isolation."[5]

The individual suffers and wanes. But, for Adorno, rather than promoting the strengthening of the individual against the mass, what matters is to understand isolation as a scar left by that which, in society, indefinitely defers the real possibility of a non-commodified individuation, and that instead commits the individual to the unalloyed identity of the ever same. From the perspective of a pending reconciliation, it would not make sense to reinforce the (false) alternative between isolation (in the self) or fusion (in the mass) – a duality modeled after the pattern of pure, unalloyed identity; rather, it is necessary to support the emergence of an individual and a collective transformed against an identitarian logic. This logic represses the multiple affinities between what exists – affinities emphasized in the mimetic impulse – in favor of the production of homogeneous interiorities, without windows, whose sole way of affirming themselves in existence depends on the possibility of insisting on their independence from others, as well as eliminating the presence of the other in the self. In that way, the Adornian critique of the individual not only exposes its subtle internal duality – ideological and emancipatory – but as it reflects on the possibility of a non-impoverished individuation, it also retraces what seemed to be its pure exteriority: the collective.

What resonances might these Adornian arguments have in our own time? Both at the political and at the ideological level, the historical moment proper to Adorno's critical analysis seems to be the reverse of our current moment. In his case, we were dealing with a "decay of the individual" promoted not only by totalitarian regimes where the manifestation of difference was directly suppressed via violent methods in the name of the collective or of *raison d'état*, but also by all the other systems where any remainder of singularity tended to collapse "peacefully" as the effect of a massive implementation of integrative policies of market amplification, which, alongside the promise of higher levels of comfort, generated homogeneity, docility, and the "conformism" of vast sectors of the population at a world scale. In the new phase of a neoliberal capitalism that is entrepreneurial and post-utopian, by contrast, what has seemed to have fallen into decay is the very promise of integration, as well as the diverse representations of a collective subject or, more broadly, of the figures that aimed to allude to dimensions of life not explainable with reference to the isolated, monadic individual.

The advent of meritocratic criteria of justice and the reconfiguration of subjectivity around the entrepreneurial ideal collaborate to form a strongly individualizing morality – a morality thanks to which the ideal neoliberal subject acquires the certainty that the only limits are those imposed by the self, thereby making the subject solely responsible for their own life and even their death. On the other hand, the ideas of a post-hegemonic neoliberalism, disorganized and anomic, project the image of a world in which the dense ideological stratification constructed by liberal humanism becomes flattened and where domination acquires a newfound literalness. What would be, then, the critical potential of a model of interrogation that submerges us in a language of individual autonomy that today seems to be the dominant ideology and, furthermore, brings into play mechanisms of interrogation – deployment of tensions and ambivalences in terms, twisting and internal transmutations of the categories that intend to name domination and emancipation – whose subtlety seems ill matched for an ideological conjuncture at once much simpler, much more literal and stark? Would it not be more appropriate to apply more direct modes of questioning, less closely attached to the paradoxical character of its object?

As I have been suggesting in this book, it is not at all obvious, however, that the thesis of a simplification of the ideological space can be taken as the necessary conclusion to the confrontation between the historical situation described by Adorno and our "incredible" present moment.[6] In reality, it is this thesis that should be interrogated in terms of its interpretive possibilities and of its ideological affinity with its own object of analysis. On the one hand, in a context where the exponential growth of inequality coexists with relatively low levels of social conflict and political opposition – when compared with, for instance, the decade prior to World War I – contemporary neoliberalism demonstrates much more than the pure, simple capacity to deploy raw violence. It demonstrates, concretely, an enormous ideological potency that allows it to articulate new moral imperatives with pre-existing social fantasies, and to operate at the level of individuals' psychic economies.

On the other hand, the diagnosis of a contemporary "simplification" of the ideological space sometimes corresponds to the thesis of a greater "transparency" of domination. Those cultural objects that an earlier criticism insisted on seeing as belaboring an internal dialectic would finally – and happily – be revealed for what they always were: mere rediscoveries of the raw reality of exploitation. But this position risks losing sight of the fact that the desire for "literality" is one of the ideological motifs criticism should attempt to problematize instead of taking it as its own ideal. As exemplified by the persistent references by the new right-wing movements to evidence drawn from everyday life, the self-evidence of people's vital interest, and the simplicity of a world situated beyond political "narratives" analyzed in chapter 2, the transparency bestowed on neoliberalism is a central component of the consciousness neoliberalism has of itself. One plainly sees this in neoliberalism's "sincerity discourse," and in its professed gambit in favor of a literality that cannot be fooled by opacities, nuance, and "philosophizing rhetoric." So, if it is true that the mere denunciation of the "false" of ideology has always found itself powerless when facing ideology itself, this becomes all the more true when it is easier to celebrate the transparency of facts in a time when literality itself has come to constitute a dominant value.

But beyond this general consideration about the recharged persistence of ideology today, it would be appropriate to suspect that the very singularities of the ideological conjuncture in which we live do not let us discard the old terms employed by Adorno's critique. In particular, what should we do with a pretension to autonomy that occupies a privileged position in the ideological configuration of our time, but whose conditions of possibility are also undermined – as we saw in chapter 2 – by the advances of an anti-intellectual neoliberalism? What should we do with a discourse of autonomy that, while fulfilling a major role in the responsibilization and incrimination of the individual carried out by neoliberalism, at the same time supports the struggles of diverse social movements as an unavoidable element of a contemporary critique of violence?

In sympathy with the paradoxical situation that, according to Adorno, critical thought faced in the 20th century in dealing with the category of the individual, the critique of neoliberalism finds itself today in a dilemma with respect to the discourse of autonomy. And this is due less to an insufficiency in thought itself and more to the objective complexity that is the motor and purview of thought itself.

Ambiguous Fragility

Appealing to a Benjaminian figure, we could say that today the discourse of autonomy constitutes simultaneously a document of culture and barbarism, a testimony which critical thought cannot "contemplate without horror"[7] but neither can it address with disdain, as if it were a mere vice of the past or of a present to overcome. By doing so, we would be contributing in no small measure to the reproduction of violence in its currently privileged forms. The persistence in the idea of autonomy alone cannot, however, justify its preservation. From an Adornian perspective, we could say that the task would be rather to work on the concept so as to bring to light certain critical profiles in order to rearrange them in a new figure.

Just as recovering the moment of truth of the category of the individual implies detaching the figure of individuality from the isolated individual with which it is usually associated, the necessary persistence in demanding autonomy must be able to inflect that notion in such a way as to delink it from other notions, such as independence and self-sufficiency.

It is along these lines that, I will suggest, Judith Butler has been working, not only in books marked quite strongly by the language of moral philosophy, as in *Giving an Account of Oneself* (2005), but also in *Precarious Life: The Powers of Mourning and Violence* (2004), *Dispossession: The Performative in the Political* (2013), and *Notes Toward a Performative Theory of Assembly* (2018), which, initially, might seem to be committed to a completely different end: to reflect on the dimensions of vulnerability and interdependence constitutive of contemporary subjectivities and that turn out to be disavowed by the ideology of autonomy imposed by neoliberalism.

In *Notes Toward a Performative Theory of Assembly*, Butler begins, in essence, a consideration of the powers of alliance between bodies that make themselves visible in public with a critical diagnosis of the normativity of contemporary neoliberalism, which, the author argues, "demands self-sufficiency as a moral ideal"[8] and positions the ideas of personal autonomy and responsibility as the centerpieces of a "cruel" discourse. According to this discourse, for instance, people who do not have jobs that provide health insurance deserve to die. Faced with this idea, Walter Benjamin would say, the critical task is to recapture astonishment as the first step in the transformation of the world that makes this situation possible and that this discourse seeks to eternalize. Along these lines, Butler writes: "The fantasy of the individual capable of undertaking entrepreneurial self-making under conditions of accelerating precarity, if not destitution, makes the uncanny assumption that people can, and must, act in autonomous ways under conditions where life has become unlivable."[9]

What is it about this neoliberal morality that is astonishing, or, as Butler puts it, uncanny? On the one hand, the idea – which has nonetheless enjoyed a notable credibility through modern history – that our acting is "originary" or that it is caused and conditioned only by itself, or that it is "autonomous" in the sense of self-sufficient. On the other hand, what is also "uncanny" is the historically produced marriage of the principle of individual self-sufficiency – which in modernity generally accompanied the idea of autonomy – with a novel production of precarity that systematically destroys the institutions, infrastructures, and foundations necessary for action across vast sectors of the population. It is this very marriage between demanding autonomy in the sense of self-sufficiency, on the one hand, *and* the systematic yet unevenly distributed precarization of life, on the other, that in an affective plane Butler associates with cruelty, a joyous cruelty which is propelled by the neoliberal appropriation of the language of ethics. But, in the author's analysis, this level – more conjunctural, if you will – never erases the other: the uncanniness of the pretense of self-sufficiency, of radical non-dependence and absolute self-reference of what exists, that turns my dependence on others into a negatively valorized accident. It is to this idea of dependence, as well as the concept's various internal differentiations, that Butler's analysis will return again and again.

In fact, in the exercise of conceptual disarticulation of this individualizing and exasperating form of responsibility that is typical of neoliberal morality, Butler emphasizes that what neoliberalism makes unthinkable is interdependence. They also introduce an internal differentiation of the concept of dependence through which we might eventually come to think an alternative ethics, associated with the solidary idea of responsibility that would "ratify our mutual dependence." Butler writes: "On the one hand, everyone is dependent on social relations and enduring infrastructure in order to maintain a livable life, so there is no getting rid of that dependency. On the other hand, that dependency, though not the same as a condition of subjugation, can easily become one."[10]

What is false about the discourse of autonomy is located, in Butler's analysis, in those two concepts that, while being related to the idea of dependence, operate at different levels, and that it is important to keep separate: on the one side, existential vulnerability and, on the other, a socially produced and unequally administered precarity. The shared vulnerability that the idea of autonomy as self-sufficiency disavows is, in reality, insurmountable and the potential starting point for a new ethics, as well as new forms of collective action. But a discourse that identifies this existential vulnerability with an imposed and unequally distributed precarity ("we are all vulnerable") is a discourse that disavows inequalities and uplifts the present insofar as it makes an unjust, contingent historical situation into an eternal condition. Conversely, "dependence," in the sense of a structural exposure *to*, vulnerability *with respect to*, and compossibility *with* others, not only is it not surmountable, but it would not be "overcome" by an alternative ethics to the subjugating dependence generated by the process of precarization. Even if it is not possible to distinguish between them *a priori*, for the sake of efforts to resist the hyper-responsibilizing morality promoted by neoliberalism, it is crucial to not collapse them into one. Existential vulnerability is not unequal, socially administered precarity. It is a matter of insisting on the distinction between the vulnerable, dependent character of our lives – irredeemably interlaced with many others – and a calculated undermining of our conditions of life that exploits such a dependence. In the first case, dependence is an index of a latent potential to be with others that could eventually be activated. In the second case, it is synonymous with subordination in a hierarchical ladder that seeks to arrange isolated individuals in order to guarantee the systematic reproduction of an unjust, unequal world.

Toward a Dialectic of Autonomy

In *Notes Toward a Performative Theory of Assembly* – as in most of Butler's books – the emphasis is on what we could conceive of as the diverse political valences of our dependencies, based on the diagnosis of neoliberalism as rendering unthinkable the very idea of interdependence. Butler does not seek to develop the idea of autonomy in an emancipatory sense. However, far from widening the distance between interdependence and autonomy, the author's reflections on the multiple ways in which we depend on others do not seek to substitute the rationalist preoccupations of moral philosophy around the individual for a semantics of an impulsive multitude, a multitude that is corporeal and radically spontaneous, or to reify it as a philosophy of homelessness. Rather, they present us with a series of dilemmas. How can we develop a critique of the currently ongoing hyper-responsibilization of the individual without renouncing the discourse of ethics in general and the ideal of responsibility in particular? How can we formulate a critique of the ideology that mandates individual self-sufficiency as moral ideal at the same time as it promotes a process of generalized precarity that structurally undermines the very possibility of self-sufficiency, without thereby appealing to a minoritizing discourse where the very inclination to organize collective action is discarded beforehand?

Faced with these dilemmas, we cannot argue for, and even less adopt, Manichean positions. Butler argues that even if it is clear that neoliberalism has appropriated the language of ethics, and that it has given a privileged status to a concept of responsibility that limits itself to the obligation of proving (to oneself) and demanding (of others) economic self-sufficiency independently of the structural conditions that actively undermine the possibility of economic self-sufficiency for vast sectors of the population, the concept of responsibility cannot be abandoned since it "remains a crucial feature of the critique of accelerating inequality."[11]

According to my own interpretation, such a situation of ambivalence, which reveals an object that simultaneously does damage and is damaged, is implicit also in Butler's argument about autonomy. Butler refers to this argument when they thematize explicitly – in line with Wendy Brown – the de-autonomizing effects of the material precarization of life that we discussed in chapter 2, but also, indirectly, when, starting from the diagnosis of an increasing material precarization, they reflect on the claims or exercises of the right to have rights carried forward by people we might consider as de-subjectified subjects: exposed to the moral imperative of self-sufficiency and, at the same time, "free" from the support that would make their lives livable.[12] Both perspectives are united in a double thesis: "none of us acts without the conditions to act, even though sometimes we must act to install and preserve those very conditions."[13] This two-pronged position poses important questions that a potential reworking of the idea of autonomy must attend to, since this position unleashes a sort of negative dialectic where, among other things, two borders of a theoretical and political abyss that we ought to avoid become glaringly visible: on the one hand, to affirm the unconditionality of autonomous action as if this were available at all times and places for everyone – regardless of an unequal distribution of the conditions necessary for action – and, on the other hand, to deduce from the diagnosis of material and psychic precarization of life that no autonomy can be expected from already precarious subjects. Let's examine this issue more closely.

The reference to the struggle for the right to have rights introduces, of course, a paradoxical idea. On the one hand, these struggles are efforts *to secure* the currently non-existent social, economic, political, and psychic conditions needed for autonomous action. But, at the same time, these struggles actualize with varying degrees of intensity that same autonomy whose historical destruction by precarization is denounced. The uneasy coexistence of both ideas does not avoid the contradiction, but in the formulation that Butler proposes – no one acts without the conditions for action, but we sometimes act to bring about those conditions – something else happens: we are alerted to the problematic character of the attempt to carry out these arguments to their ultimate conclusions. By claiming that none of us acts without the conditions that enable our action, one seeks to disentangle the ideological nexus between autonomous action and self-sufficiency: all autonomous action, in order to exist, is in reality actually dependent, insofar as it is prepared by certain conditions whose absence would threaten the possibility of autonomy. However, from this critical argument we must not conclude – as a conservative paternalism has tended to hold in relation to popular sectors – that until the conditions for autonomous action are given, no autonomous action is possible and that, therefore, as the logical consequence of the process of precarization of life, we face a situation of consummate de-subjectification that particularly afflicts the most socioeconomically precarious sectors of the population. The second part of Butler's statement alerts us to this ideological, paternalistic drift. Interrupting the linear causality that the economicist argument might introduce, their argument reminds us that *even though* there is no such thing as unconditioned action, *sometimes* we act to bring about those conditions. So, the first part of the argument does not disappear, but it is subjected to a rewriting: while remaining legible, it becomes de-absolutized while marking the fatalist drift which even critical thought (not to mention conservative thought) can veer toward. Conversely, the emphasis on the material conditioning of all action interrupts the idealist and falsely universalizing voluntarism that could become prominent should the idea reassert itself that there is political action even when the conditions for it are missing. This emphasis reminds us that the emergence of struggles over the necessary conditions for autonomous action is a fragile possibility that must be articulated politically, and on which we cannot count as if we were dealing with a *fatum* that will impose itself "despite everything" thanks to the perennial, resilient power of the multitude.

Starting from this inevitably complex position, one might produce an interesting updating of the Adornian critique we discussed earlier on the matter of the individual. This argument might allow us to think against a presupposition of personal autonomy that hyper-responsibilizes subjects while making them disposable, unstable composites of gestures of autonomy and experiences of shared vulnerability as the basis for a new type of collective action and a new type of solidarity, attempting to avoid both political fatalism and political voluntarism. Effectively, even though Butler's argument does not emphasize such a re-elaboration, it does suggest a crucial question for the development of a transfigured sense of the idea of autonomy:

does autonomy, as a certain capacity of agency, really have an antithetical relation to dependence? Or is it rather neoliberalism's hyper-responsibilizing morality – and, more fundamentally, a certain dominant tendency in Western thought – that exploits the antithesis between autonomy and dependence, fomenting the fantasy of free action as necessarily independent, egoistic, detached, self-referential, and self-founding? If the latter is the case, perhaps it would be worth thinking that autonomy – as was the case with Adorno's critique of the isolated individual and his idea of individuation associated with mimesis that was not antithetical to the collective – is not just another current political problem, but can also become inflected in different ways. Actually, it is precisely at the moment when the individualist, isolationist version of autonomy becomes articulated in new formulations that reach unsuspected levels of cruelty that the production of new and more emancipatory inflections becomes crucial.

The materialist critique rejects the abstract, eternal, self-referential conditionals that formal logic imposes. It does not argue that *if* we exalt autonomy, *then* we defend freedom. But it also does not say the opposite. Rather, it submits its own reasoning to what history has produced so far and could still produce in the future. It says: *given* that even when it figures quite prominently in the neoliberal morality, autonomy constitutes one of the elements that has been profoundly damaged by neoliberal precarization, it is necessary to sharpen our ears to hear the truth implicit in the concept at the very moment of its effective decay. What is at stake, then, from the point of view of critical theory is not so much to decide if we should think with or against autonomy *tout court*, but how we are to inflect the concept. Whether we do so in the constellation of self-sufficiency that figures me as solely responsible for my actions, and where the presupposition of autonomy tends to feed the punitive matrix of neoliberalism; or whether, in opposition to neoliberalism, we commit to inflections – both theoretical and political – of autonomy in the constellation of vulnerability in order to make it work alongside a new idea of collectivity, against precarization. In this new valence, autonomy could be the name for the singular potential that does not oppose but feeds on the existing interdependencies, without reifying, however, the current collective being – through a reflexive process that is corporeally situated and that enables new conjunctions hitherto unthinkable. Autonomy could also name the pressure – immanent to this collectivity – toward the realization of historical opportunities whose possibilities were shut off by reality, or rather toward the creation of what is yet to be, through a process of simultaneous activation and stirring of current interdependencies.

5

Neoliberal Sensibilities

> Through emotions, the past persists on the surface of bodies. Emotions show us how histories stay alive, even when they are not consciously remembered; how histories of colonialism, slavery, and violence shape lives and worlds in the present.
>
> Sara Ahmed, *The Cultural Politics of Emotion*[1]

Neoliberalism has often been associated with an individualist doctrine and a process of de-solidarization, fundamentally objectionable due to its privatizing and atomizing consequences in social life. However, the emergence of neoliberal governments that are simultaneously deregulatory in the economic sphere *and* disciplinarian or plainly authoritarian in the sphere of politics and culture presents a two-pronged challenge for ideology critique: the task of problematizing the supposed commitment of neoliberal ideology to individual autonomy, and to highlight the anti-democratic slant in the way subjects are called to answer the entrepreneurial mandate of omnipotence under conditions of growing subjective powerlessness. This chapter wishes to contribute to the understanding of Argentine neoliberalism by attending to that double challenge, first, by reconstructing the neoliberal drift of the notion of justice and freedom elaborated by François Dubet and Wendy Brown, and, second, by analyzing the more or less unconscious ideological substratum in which local neoliberal discourses found a fertile ground to root.

Even though no attempt to conceptualize Argentine neoliberalism can do without the persistent critical analysis of subjective models and figures of life in common projected from within the political system by various government discourses, I believe that the understanding and mapping of anti-democratic processes (both political and cultural) that have grown sharper in recent years also require the critical interpretation of a certain social sensibility which is older and more ambivalent. Not reducible *to* and yet encouraging *of* new ideological articulations promoted by discourses of the new right-wing formations, this social sensibility constitutes, to my understanding, the distinctive matter onto which these discourses could and can latch, and its consideration likewise suggests certain limitations in the diagnosis of our present as enveloped in that technocratic de-politicization forged in the context of the neoliberal 1990s. Keeping in view this political and social dimension of ongoing processes, it is important to articulate a theoretical-political focus with a more sociological view, whose relevance lies, not in the last instance, in enabling a conception of neoliberalism as a complex of *productive* political forces that are simultaneously *expressive* of a given state of society, rather than a pure demiurgic force.

Among the many legible folds of that social sensibility, which has been increasingly influential since the end of the 2000s, I am particularly interested in two issues that, I think, must be considered simultaneously. On the one hand, I focus on the inflections of personal autonomy that are predominantly conceivable in the context of that sensibility. On the other hand, I consider the representations of justice that this sensibility enables and to which it binds itself. I think that considering both aspects simultaneously would give credit to the hypothesis that Argentine Macrismo represents a politicization of a pre-existing anti-democratic sensibility. In defining personal autonomy exclusively in terms of self-sufficiency and individual self-valuation, while simultaneously articulating an experience of injustice in terms of a demand for meritocratic redistribution or for security, this anti-democratic sensibility encouraged the political identification of the (self-)problematization of the present and the calls for social justice that gained prominence during the 2000s with a pathological negativity that had to be rejected in favor of the reinstatement of a lost order.

Late Capitalism and Models of Justice

According to Wolfgang Streeck, with the end of the Cold War and the revamping of capitalist relations of production during the 1970s, there was an inflection point in the hitherto relatively harmonious link between capitalism and democracy, which had been in place since the end of World War II. If in economic terms that harmonic coexistence, accomplished under the pressure of social struggles, was based in a Keynesian model of promoting growth by redistribution from the top to the bottom, the "Hayek model" that would become its replacement would set its sights on redistribution from the bottom to the top. This upward redistribution had enormous de-democratizing effects in political as well as ideological terms. At a political level, this model demanded of its ruling parties a renewed effort at shielding themselves from constituents and affiliates, which favored – even if it was not its only cause – a tendency to political disaffiliation. At an ideological level, it fomented a process of de-solidarization by which every policy oriented toward minimizing the growing social inequality was deemed redundant or even noxious. This process, according to Streeck, promoted the widespread cynical attitude toward a capitalism that had given up pretending it would develop a just society and that limited itself to "founding *social integration* on *collective resignation* as the last remaining pillar of the capitalist social order, or disorder."[2]

Even if it is not at all evident that the revamping of capitalism since the 1970s could be conceptualized as a plain "abandonment" of its normative pretensions in favor of the sheer imposition of forceful arrangements favorable to capital, analyses of that moment of inflexion (from the most diverse sources) agree with Streeck's argument in pointing out that the diffusion not only of ideas but also of a certain sensibility that opposes welfare policies promoted by the social state constitutes one of the clearest throughlines of the cultural neoliberalism which has been dominant since that moment. Thus, even while they disagree with Streeck's diagnosis of "anomie" that his argument tends to suggest,[3] writers as different as François

Dubet and Wendy Brown converge in seeing the downfall, under neoliberalism, of the idea of social justice, understood as something more than simple equality of opportunity to compete in the capitalist market and proper self-valorization. This idea of social justice, which had been crucial to democratizing struggles throughout the 20th century, underwent a process of transformation, whereby it supposedly became either a conservative idea or synonymous with an illegitimate intervention, when not just plain unadulterated totalitarianism.

In several of his books, Dubet returns to the political challenges that the idea of social justice – understood as equity of positions in the social structure and the closing of the gap between the poorest and the richest – faced in the 20th century. He also discusses its overshadowing by the idea of equality of opportunities and he analyzes the consequences of that process for democracy. Distancing himself from the diagnosis of generalized cynicism as a feature of neoliberalism, Dubet understands the revindications in favor of one or another model of equality as appeals to two different models of justice, whose difference he underscores with reference to the game of musical chairs. If equality of positions, associated with the classic concept of social justice, argues over the number of chairs, the second model tries to find the best way to occupy existing positions while observing a persistent silence vis-à-vis the ever-dwindling reduction and unilaterally emphasizing the role of personal merit in the quest for the goal. The exaltation of personal autonomy, understood as self-sufficiency, constitutes therefore a *locus classicus* of the model of equality of opportunities "that always seems to say, in the end, that one doesn't owe anything to anyone, [forgetting that] the success of the few would not have been possible without the collective capital of infrastructures, of teams, of culture, and of the institutions that have allowed them to profit from their talents."[4]

Even though they are both related to the issue of justice, for Dubet, the social value and the ethical-political potency of these two models are substantially different. The "justice of positions" is, on the one hand, more generous than equality of opportunities because it does not allow us to forget what we owe others: "it remembers that the production of winners does not demand the sacrifice of the vanquished."[5] But also, and simultaneously, if liberalism is defined by its claim to favor the development of individual autonomy, this justice is also more liberal because – Dubet writes in sympathy with what we have seen in previous chapters – despite the claims of the predominant common sense, the justice of positions defends in the best way possible the search for individual autonomy: "I am all the more free to act when I'm not threatened by enormous social inequality."[6] "Rethinking social justice" entails, then, getting involved in a reflection that points in two different directions that may seem contradictory in our time. It is not just a question of underlining how much we have in common with others in opposition to the process of de-solidarization launched by the neoliberal rewiring of capitalism. It is also necessary to do justice to the promise of individual autonomy that, despite its self-representation, that very neoliberalism is incapable of sustaining, insofar as it undermines the material conditions of production of subjective autonomy.

What does this neoliberal self-representation entail, and what is the meaning of the images of liberty and justice that it projects? To what extent are these images actually a part of the lived experience and the sensibility of subjects in contemporary societies? The present chapter endeavors to tackle these questions. But before continuing along these lines, it is worth highlighting the value of the theoretical-critical impulse behind such an investigation: the resistance to the injunction to remain *inside* the given conjuncture, leaving its sense intact and adopting its terms. Instead of taking as one's own the alternative *between* autonomy and solidarity/social justice, pointing to the double value of what Dubet has called "the justice of positions" allows us to envision that alternative as already something projected by neoliberal ideology, whose deconstruction would not only be an important element of the *political* struggles over democracy in the present, but also be a necessary point of departure in order to make *intelligible* the increasing authoritarianism of contemporary neoliberalism.

From a political perspective, the deconstruction of the alternative between autonomy and solidarity/social justice is relevant for democracy because said alternative encourages a dissociation – an opposition even – of, on the one hand, the current struggles for economic equality and, on the other, the protest movements that problematize different dominant forms of heteronomy and dependence that have been socially imposed and administered, thus undermining the possible alliances between politically active social collectives. This dissociation removes in advance the sense of autonomy in question from the arena of political debate. Understood as asymptotic in relation to the claim for a social justice to come, "autonomy" can only mean a self-sufficient positivity that "already knows what it wants," and not, for example, the subjective potential never fully guaranteed by a persistent questioning of the given, which resists the absolutization of the present and the annulment of critical impulses, promoted in an ever more explicit way by neoliberal governments, whether as official discourse, or through the repression or judicialization of protest.

But on the other hand, the deconstruction of the alternative between autonomy and social justice is fundamental also as it concerns the possibility of *understanding* the genre of neoliberalism currently alive and well in Latin America and other countries. Given that such an alternative tends to assume as a given neoliberalism's commitment to the autonomy of individuals – eventually finding objectionable only its atomizing social effects – its currency becomes an obstacle for conceptualizing contemporary neoliberalism insofar as it renders radically unimaginable the possibility of neoliberalism's conservative or even reactionary inflection from a politico-cultural perspective. In effect, how would we explain the injunctions to submit to the order of things and present-day hierarchies, the tendencies to punish and to self-punish, to unlimited punitivism and sacrifice, that actually existing neoliberalism does not cease to exacerbate if we start from the position that neoliberalism is essentially associated with a spirit of "tolerance" of diversity and with the defense of subjective autonomy? To consider escalating anti-gender discourse and the crusade-like spirit that marks the current practices of many right-wing political movements all over the world as mere *reactions to* neoliberalism or as *deviations from* its "logic" would imply the acritical reproduction of neoliberalism's own self-representation, one that obtains its purity from the projection of inverted specular identities (for example, populism). Insofar as it is *imaginary*, this self-representation is, moreover, unable to conceptualize the not necessarily harmonic or coherent internal complexity of these ideologies.

So, rather than persisting in a dichotomous, purist frame as our reading strategy, the critical understanding of the present requires returning to the alternative between autonomy and social justice so as to interrogate it as an effect of a culture already structured in a neoliberal key. That is, to approach it as one of the many artifacts produced by neoliberalism, which, behind the opposition of these terms, hides a profoundly conservative dimension of this ideology which can combine, without contradiction, anti-egalitarian policies of deregulation, familialism, and the promotion of political authoritarianism.

Conservative Deregulation: "The Neoliberal Frankenstein"

> I want to give France its freedom back. I want to take it out of jail.
>
> Marine Le Pen, April 2017[7]

Wendy Brown proceeds in this deconstructive vein as she takes apart the common-sense valences of "liberal" in neoliberalism, in a text where she not only demonstrates the demonization of social justice spearheaded by doctrinaire authors such as Hayek but also interrogates the conceptions of liberty and justice that undergird the rejection. Here Brown exposes a neoliberalism that is not "anomic" but, rather, socioculturally conservative, and that early on called for an "expansion of the private," shedding new light on the seeming impossibility of an authoritarian neoliberalism that, nonetheless, appears to be actualized in different contemporary political experiences.

For someone like Hayek, Brown argues, "social justice" is tyrannical or fascist. The charge levied at political projects that advance social justice is not only that they serve goals that are egalitarian rather than libertarian, but also that by intervening politically they work against the spontaneous market order and the "personal, protected sphere" – seeking to control, or introducing noise and *political* disagreements into, the "harmonic" evolution of private life. According to the canonical author of classical neoliberalism, freedom only blooms where politics – understood as the regulation and public problematization of reasons, interests, sensibilities, and arguments in conflict – is absent, and justice emerges as a dangerous concept when, as is the case with the term "social justice," it is applied to the condition of a State or a people. Any curtailing of freedom[8] in the name of civility, equality, inclusion, public goods, and, even more, the "dangerous superstition" of social justice is located, for Hayek, in a continuum with fascism and totalitarianism, while deregulation and privatization emerge as unlimited moral and philosophical principles that extend beyond the economic sphere.[9]

Developing this last point, Brown shows that the privatization spearheaded by neoliberalism does not limit itself to the privatization or dismantling of public goods and services or to the concomitant meritocratic hyper-responsibilization of the individual for their survival; privatization here also implies an attempt to expand the "personal, protected sphere" in order to restrict the reach of politics and to undermine properly social claims. To privatize means, in this second sense, to designate as "private" an increasing number of activities and therefore to deregulate and shield them from democratic norms such as equality, inclusivity, access, civility, and tolerance. In the case of the United States, this means, for instance, that individual and civil rights such as freedom of opinion or religious freedom can be extended to corporations, in such a way that these can be shielded from political regulation that would otherwise limit various forms of discriminatory practices. But the same privatization – which in extending individual rights hitherto attributed to people to corporations ends up challenging egalitarian, anti-discriminatory principles and practices – produces also, Brown claims, a familialization of the public. The expansion of the sheltered personal sphere becomes a way to introduce family values into public spaces hitherto structured by democratic norms and laws, which not only threatens the principles of equality, secularism, pluralism, and inclusivity at the heart of modern democratic society but also seeks to replace those principles with traditional moral values drawn from "the personal, protected sphere." In this way, in an ironic twist particularly for those who claim to want to leave the "paternalistic"[10] State behind,

> expanding the "personal, protected sphere" and curtailing the reach of democracy in the name of freedom develops a new ethos of the nation, one that replaces a public, pluralistic, secular democratic national imaginary with a private, homogenous, familial one. [. . .] When the twin dimensions of privatization we have been considering

> [economic and ethical] discursively capture the nation itself, it ceases to be figured primarily as a democracy but instead is figured as a competitive business needing to make good deals and attract investors, on the one hand, and as an inadequately secured home, besieged by ill-willed or non-belonging outsiders, on the other.[11]

The development of the thesis according to which there is a traditionalist moralism that is part and parcel of doctrinaire neoliberalism and not a mere "deviation" from its logic constitutes an important point of departure to understand the reality of contemporary neoliberalism and the imbrication of de-democratizing tendencies that it simultaneously expresses and makes possible. In Brown's argument, these de-democratizing tendencies inscribed in neoliberal doctrine acquire a double valence. If the economic privatization ushered in by neoliberalism turns out to be profoundly subversive of democracy because it generates, among other things, forms of exclusion and inequality, and turns public goods into private property, the privatized ethos – exclusive, homogeneous, hierarchical, authoritarian – that neoliberalism promotes likewise undermines democracy since it fans the flames of a familial, traditionalist morality that is particularly germane for the development of xenophobic, misogynistic, punitive political formations.

So, whereas the uncritical reproduction of the unified, imaginary self-representation projected by neoliberalism renders unthinkable – or thinkable only as radical exteriorities – forms of xenophobia, racism, and LGBTQ+phobia that are deeply embedded in our contemporaneity, Brown's disentangling of the double valences of the privatization of life – economic and ethical – as proposed by the theorists of classical neoliberalism helps us to navigate one of the great "mysteries" of our present: how is it possible that the Right today can be advertised and perceived as, simultaneously, the party of liberty *and* order? The critique of neoliberalism that exposes the imbrication of economic deregulation, cultural conservatism, and the potential for political authoritarianism in classical neoliberal doctrine demonstrates that the mystery of a libertarian discipline or a libertarian and authoritarian conservatism is not so mysterious after all, and, thus, that the new political right-wing movements that rehearse its terms can surely not be called democratic given the kind of sociability they promote.

But if this critique greatly contributes to our conceptualization of doctrinal neoliberalism's internal complexity and helps us to unravel a few of the common-sensical notions that often shield governments from criticism, this critique is also not sufficient for our understanding of our present in ideological terms. To what extent do these neoliberal self-representations of liberty and justice constitute active elements in contemporary sensibilities? One cannot, in fact, deduce from the existence of an ideology as doctrine the possibility of its existence as viable political articulation in a given historical moment. Even less can one deduce a real ideology as *lived experience* on the part of its subjects, that is, as a web of common sense and affects that are central to the reproduction and transformation of societies, and that can be understood neither as subjective responses to the objects' intrinsic natural attributes – the phenomenological temptation – nor as stemming from subjectivity – the psychological temptation. For this reason, in order to produce an interpretation of neoliberalism as political and social reality, we must complement Brown's disentangling of the double valence of privatization in neoliberal doctrine with a concrete analysis of the political formations and the social sensibilities that experiment, endure, and act through that double register.

Neoliberal Sensibilities in 21st-Century Argentina

> I can tell you about democracy in terms of my freedom. I'm free to buy this or that product in the supermarket, but I feel that I don't even have that freedom anymore. [. . .] In fact, the menu today, unless you make anywhere from 25,000 to 30,000 pesos, is the menu of the *precios cuidados*, what the president wants you to eat; that's not democracy.
>
> Interview conducted in Buenos Aires, January 2015[12]

In Argentina, the coexistence of discourses that exalted the virtues of a deregulated life – free from the "artificially imposed" strictures on the "incessant initiatives" of an individual imagined as infinitely entrepreneurial – and the calls for a re-establishment of a "lost order" – which pontificated on the virtues of austerity and diminishing expectations of citizens about the rights the

State should guarantee – became a characteristic feature of the interpellations propelled by the government of Alianza Cambiemos under the presidency of Mauricio Macri (2015–19). The rhetoric of Macrismo could bring together, without contradiction, the affirmation of the "unlimited power" of all *and* the call to "sincerely" recognize the necessary sacrifice we all had to make after a time of "moral chaos." Appealing to the images of a reproachable degradation that had to be left behind, the discourse of a restored freedom that could now appropriately restore to each individual full responsibility for their destiny was mixed in with the irresponsible reproduction of old social prejudices against immigrants, precarious sectors of the population, and social activists, generally characterized as "lazy" or as deserters from a competitive struggle "full of opportunities" for self-valorization.[13]

But this articulation of atomizing libertarianism *and* punitivism that is today recognizable across the region, and that the official discourse of Argentina's Macrismo promoted with its complaints of the supposedly heavy inheritance left by previous social policies and its moral emphasis on the need for humility and sincerity, was not a political creation *ex nihilo*. The political point of inflection represented by the new right-wing governments in the region is rooted in older ideological tendencies of international reach, tendencies that the Latin American progressive governments did not manage to reverse and that, in the case of Argentina, became manifest in the diffusion of a certain social sensibility in which, even before the coming to power of Macrismo, one could appreciate the double meaning of privatization oriented simultaneously toward restricting politics and undoing social claims, as Brown conceptualized with respect to the classical neoliberal doctrine.

As the epigraph in this section seeks to show, drawn from an investigation of anti-democratic dispositions in Argentina that began in 2011, the spread of neoliberalism as lived experience of subjects in the subtle interstices of everyday life was less an effect than a condition of possibility of the political articulation crystallized in Alianza Cambiemos and its electoral triumph in 2015. Understood as a spontaneous ideology, neoliberalism does not resemble a coherent doctrine, nor can it be seamlessly "applied" to each and every circumstance that makes up the course of an individual's life. The elements that affirm the existence of neoliberal subjectivity should be sought not in the explicit defense of both a privatizing libertarianism and a conservative discipline as two parts of the same body of ideas, but rather in a certain affective disposition more or less unconscious, porous, open, and/or receptive to a double decoding. On the one hand, the decoding of the attempts to politically regulate the market and of the redistributive policies spearheaded by the Cristina Fernández governments as shameless, inadmissible violations of intimacy that, in this discursive field, were denounced as "authoritarian political meddling" – an excess of control – in the most intimate dimensions of individuals' lives.[14] On the other hand, and yet simultaneously, the perception of that political moment as a chaotic situation – an excess of anarchy – in which traditional hierarchies and values wobbled dangerously, and which called for a reinstatement of order, for returning hierarchies to society and natural harmony to households that allegedly had been deprived of them by political debates about the meaning of democracy and the necessary rights therein.

In this neoliberal sensibility, possibly widespread from way back but accentuated in Argentina since the uproar about increasing taxes on agricultural products,[15] the deregulation demanded in the name of freedom and autonomous action coexisted quite happily with a call for more authority and more control that would allow – as Nancy Fraser puts it – sorting the capable-and-competitive wheat from the incapable-and-non-competitive chaff,[16] and that would likewise enable moral condemnation and punishment – even via physical violence – of whoever dared to defy the value of order and meritocracy as the central backbone of the political community. This two-pronged decodification, libertarian *and* authoritarian, which celebrates a personal autonomy supposedly under threat by fiscal, redistributive policies, *and* defends conservative cultural values, was expressed negatively and synthetically in one of the focus groups conducted in the context of the aforementioned investigation.[17] According to one of the participants, Kirchnerism could be described as an "anarchic authoritarianism" from whose yoke one had to become *free* in order to, paradoxically, reinstate in a social collective that had been "degrading" since 1983 – that is, since the election of the first president after the last civil–military dictatorship in Argentina – a healthy *submission* to traditional authority.

The punitive/authoritarian content of such "libertarian" demands voiced categorically here as a need to put an end, no matter the cost, to the "anarchic authoritarianism that governs us" was not exclusive to these expressions of political authoritarianism. In a more naïve fashion, unconscious or rather less politically informed, this punitivism was also made manifest in the declarations of a group of young participants who, asked to discuss the meaning of the term "social justice," did not grant it any power to limit social inequalities and, in fact, identified it without too much trouble with what is popularly known as "lynching": according to their own terms, the "justice of the people" or "justice outside of the law"; in other words, the set of violent acts "spontaneously" performed in public as a response to cases of so-called "insecurity" on the part of people who sought – legitimately from the point of view of the participants – retribution from delinquents.[18]

Far from being limited to an aggression addressed to an outside, however, this will to discipline and punish "others," which in the case of young people seemed to be associated with a certain non-representability of social justice as critical instantiation of socially imposed inequalities, became combined, in the interviews we conducted, with an exaltation of personal sacrifice and the valorization of merit as the sole just criterion of retribution.[19] Alongside austerity and a self-imposed restraint, the willingness to "tighten one's belt" was broadcast by several of the people surveyed as an index of a moral superiority, showing that they, unlike the stigmatized recipients of welfare, who were figured as morally inferior, really did know how to surmount difficult moments. "Unemployed and proud of not collecting social benefits" is how one of the participants from the middle sectors we surveyed described himself, thereby articulating this disposition to sacrifice and punishment at once. This person also spontaneously offered the interpretation previously cited of the "*precios cuidados*" program that was implemented during the second Cristina Fernández administration with the goal of setting reference prices for basic goods and that, according to him, was proof of the former president's brazen authoritarianism. Rather than an infrastructure that more or less enables a certain autonomy insofar as it attempts to limit the pressures of a quasi-monopolized market on prices, this program aroused the suspicion of the participant, who experienced it as a threat to that very autonomy. Or, as Brown would put it, he suspected a political intrusion in that "personal, protected sphere," an intrusion that sought to dictate even something as intimate as the everyday diet of Argentine families. But that "suspicion" was more than a small inkling bestowed by doctrinal reasoning. Emotionally charged, through that suspicion the program was described as a source of vexation, and its architects as rapists whose assault on life had to be repelled, at all costs and through any means necessary.[20]

These manifestations, at once libertarian and disciplinarian, which certainly challenge our traditional political parameters and dichotomies, constitute one of the productive symptoms of an ideological constellation that it would be reductive to call a pure "invention" created by new political maneuverings. Rather, the understanding that sees attempts to regulate the market via politics as inappropriate "authoritarian intrusions of politics" in one's life, and the simultaneous moral panic at situations that problematize pre-existing criteria of symbolic recognition and material distribution, are both rooted in a two-pronged affective decoding, which has been fairly generalized: autonomy as an eternal faculty of the individual, foreign to social conditions, and justice in anti-egalitarian, meritocratic, and punitive terms, according to which order constitutes the supreme value and is identified with the distribution of rewards and punishments following the sole criterion of individual performance.

In this ideological constellation, which we will proceed to sketch in what follows – based on statistical data collected through a poll conducted in the aforementioned study in Buenos Aires in 2013 – we find a dominant subjective position that:

1. tends to perceive itself as untethered from trans-subjective bonds in the pursuit of goals and where individual autonomy is not only positively linked to ideas of self-sufficiency and personal effort but also linked, negatively, to an alterity systematically perceived as threatening (whether we're referring to other individuals who threaten one's own position, or fiscal policies seen as intrusive, totalitarian, or discouraging of personal effort);
2. is oriented less toward cynicism or instrumental rationality than to a strong conventionalism about values and a submissive

position toward authority, which involves the demand for an unquestioned respect for religious and familial authority; and
3. subscribes to positions where justice acquires a meritocratic sense – according to which effort or personal sacrifice constitutes the only valid criterion to organize material retribution or symbolic recognition – or a punitive sense, generalizing the necessity of punishment and freeing it from all manner of social regulation, in the search for order and security, ultimately the supreme social values.

This "dominant subjective position" – in the sense that it represents more than 50% of the cases we analyzed – does not constitute *the* position *of* a subject in the double sense that the subject does not necessarily recognize themselves in that position, nor do they recognize the convergence of those attachments as adding up to *a* position. What we are calling the "dominant subjective position" combines elements of negative autonomism, cultural conservatism, meritocracy, and punitivism that can only be expressed *indirectly* through statements formulated in such a way as to prevent the use of general terms (of widespread positive connotation) from hampering the expression of desires and fears that perhaps the subjects were not ready to consciously claim as their own.[21] So, even if they express the same tendency, the difference between the degree of adherence with respect to the more explicit statements and those that are more indirect[22] is indicative of the distance between ideology at the doctrinal level studied by Wendy Brown, and the more diffuse affirmation at a more spontaneous ideological level, which operates in the subject in a very intense manner that is nonetheless fundamentally opaque at the level of consciousness.[23]

The same can be said about the mixing of elements. The high level of existing correlation between the majority of these statements suggests that, in this dominant subjectivity, the inflection of justice in a neoliberal key – that is, the lived experience of what is just as a retribution of merit, as the quotient of personal sacrifice invested, or as satisfaction of the imperious desire for punishment of those situated outside of order – is quite strongly linked to the adherence to traditional values and the subjective perception of individual autonomy as self-sufficiency.[24] But rather than in the mode of propositions coherently interlaced in a body of ideas positively affirmed, the constitutive elements

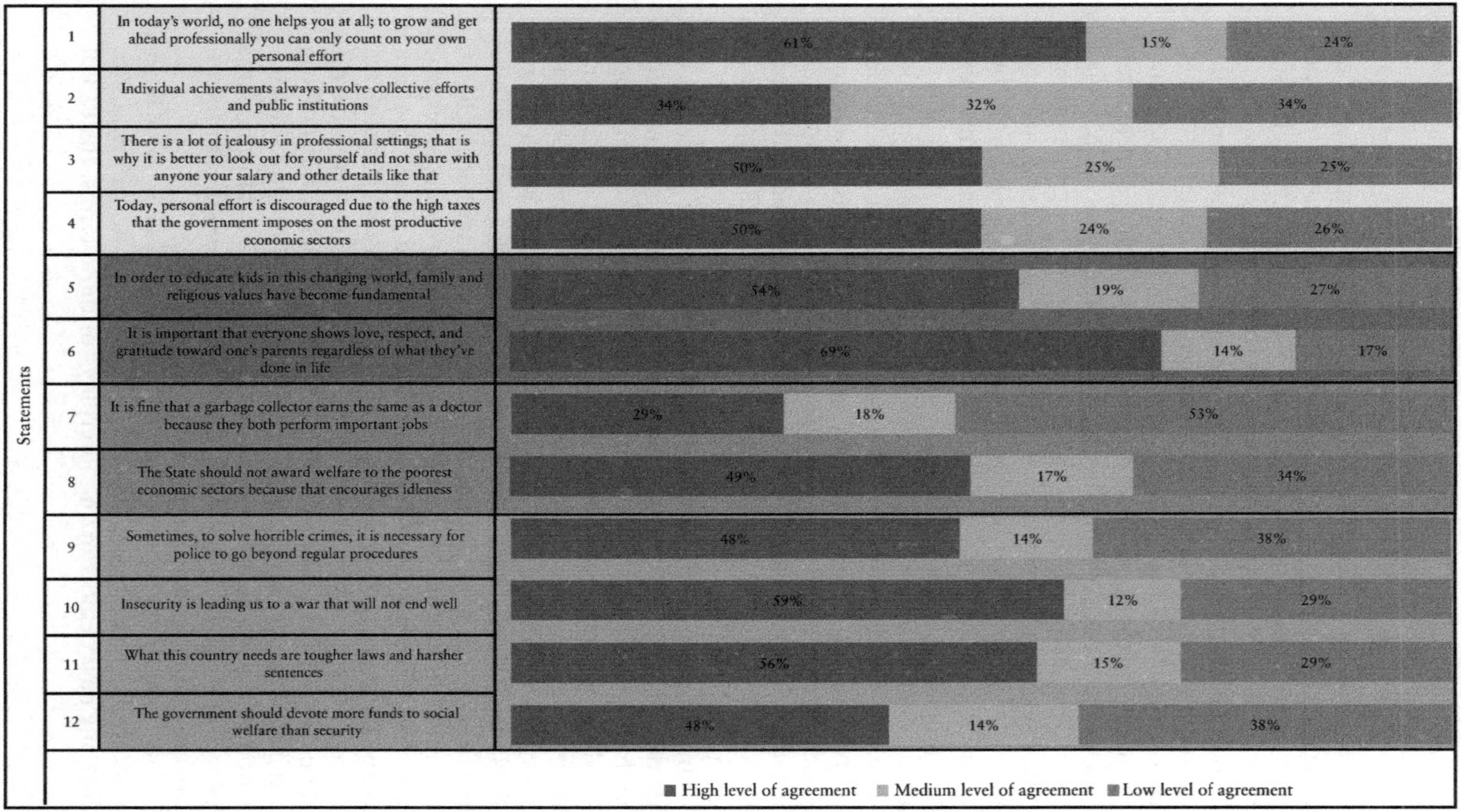
Statements
1
In today's world, no one helps you at all; to grow and get ahead professionally you can only count on your own personal effort
61%
15%
24%
2
Individual achievements always involve collective efforts and public institutions
34%
32%
34%
3
There is a lot of jealousy in professional settings; that is why it is better to look out for yourself and not share with anyone your salary and other details like that
50%
25%
25%
4
Today, personal effort is discouraged due to the high taxes that the government imposes on the most productive economic sectors
50%
24%
26%
5
In order to educate kids in this changing world, family and religious values have become fundamental
54%
19%
27%
6
It is important that everyone shows love, respect, and gratitude toward one's parents regardless of what they've done in life
69%
14%
17%
7
It is fine that a garbage collector earns the same as a doctor because they both perform important jobs
29%
18%
53%
8
The State should not award welfare to the poorest economic sectors because that encourages idleness
49%
17%
34%
9
Sometimes, to solve horrible crimes, it is necessary for police to go beyond regular procedures
48%
14%
38%
10
Insecurity is leading us to a war that will not end well
59%
12%
29%
11
What this country needs are tougher laws and harsher sentences
56%
15%
29%
12
The government should devote more funds to social welfare than security
48%
14%
38%
High level of agreement
Medium level of agreement
Low level of agreement

Source: author, drawing on «Problemas de la democracia argentina» (CONICET-FONCyT, 2013).

of what we're calling the "dominant subjective position" are interweaved here, as it were, "behind" the subject, in a manner obscure to themselves, and charged with an affective intensity that awakens passionate reactions and attachments.

It is to refer to this *productive* unconscious, in the sense that it enables certain political translations while disabling others, that we spoke of a neoliberal *sensibility* – rather than a doctrinal position – as the social substratum onto which the political interpellations of the new neoliberal governments could latch, which they then also enhanced, but couldn't create out of nothing. Macrismo in particular represented, as far as we are concerned, not so much the corollary to a growing de-politicization, but politicization of a pre-existing neoliberal sensibility that was found in large swaths of the population. It was a politicization that Macrismo managed to translate into defensive, fatalist demands for deregulation, adaptation to the established order, and repression of social protest, as well as into a general obfuscation of the complex of interdependencies in which individual experience is enmeshed, anxieties of abandonment and uncertainty generated by an increasingly unequal, hostile capitalism on a world scale.

In a more general vein, we could say that the processes of de-democratization that our societies face are associated not only with phenomena of privatizing atomization or de-solidarization – which are often the focus of our attention – but also with that which it would be too facile to consider its very opposite: processes of authoritarian de-autonomization by which hyper-flexibilized individuals, too well adapted to the system's demands, see their power to act diminished to a mere management of life in the prevailing order and under conditions of growing economic precarity. The pure antithesis of autonomy and justice does not allow us to comprehend this genre of sociopolitical phenomena, among other reasons because it does not allow us to perceive the damage that the de-democratizing processes wreak not only on equality but also on the very possibility of autonomy – understood as an open process, never guaranteed, of affirming the power to act in the web of life that exceeds us and that problematizes what is socially given.

But from a political perspective perhaps what is even more concerning is that this dichotomy also does not allow us to imagine new democratizing interplays of those terms. Instead of conceiving of claims of autonomy and justice as conclusive ideas that close in on themselves, ideas whose positive or negative value for democratic life can be ascertained independently, we should delve deeper, without dogmatism, as we consider their changing meaning in specific political articulations, and imagine diverse interplays capable of promoting a more democratic sociability. As the struggles over a new foreign debt and the struggles on behalf of workers, women, LGBTQ+, and human rights in Argentina made clear, the democratizing potential of our Latin American societies seems to lie, effectively, in *articulated* renewals of the claims for both effective autonomy and social justice, rather than in favor of one at the other's expense. In these movements, the opposition to growing economic precarity and the economization of life that makes such autonomy impossible, and the opposition to anti-intellectual tendencies that make the present absolute while pathologizing the critical impulses associated with the reflexive powers of the subject, were inseparable from the demands for social justice, which highlighted the interdependencies that sustain individual life, as well as the political responsibilities implied in the unequal distribution of a socially administered precarity.

6
Authoritarian Neoliberalism and the National Question

It is necessary to dispel the aura of impenetrability surrounding the so-called "mystery" of contemporary neoliberalism, a system that deregulates while remaining authoritarian and punitive, if we want to move beyond the self-representations projected by neoliberal ideology and engage in a critique of the authoritarian social sensibilities it manages to interpellate. As we saw in previous chapters, tracing an opposition between cultural conservatism and a libertarianism of interiority, social justice and individual autonomy, individualism and community, is itself ideological and must be subject to critique. This is not because the political challenges that these terms endeavor to index have ceased to be relevant, but rather because by setting up these oppositions we sidestep what is genuinely paradoxical and uncanny about a libertarian de-subjection of the individual that consecrates their most intimate impulses to the uncritical reproduction of the status quo while soliciting a primary narcissism; about a conservatism that does not even concern itself with the reproduction of life; and about a "community of entrepreneurs" constituted around competition and the injunction to self-valorize.

Only seen against the light, spectrally or radiographically – as Ezequiel Martínez Estrada would put it[1] – does this neoliberal imaginary of the community lose its familiarity and reveal its underside as the community of (self-)sacrifice and punishment (of others) in an absolutized present. The emergence of new aggressive nationalisms that assert the superiority of their nation over others constitutes one of the privileged forms in which this sinister dimension, punitive and authoritarian, of contemporary neoliberalism has become manifest, shielding the population from the experience of its own dispensability in the world today, and configuring it as a community of hatred adapted to the systemic imperatives of capitalism. However, at the same time, the intellectual gesture that would tend to see these self-aggrandizing nationalist impulses as the universal form of expression of this openly punitive inflection of neoliberal capitalism would be problematic, insofar as it would render invisible other forms in which authoritarian punitivism manifests itself in different regions of the world and that do not necessarily mix well with the nationalist aspirations current in many core countries. Or is it that the *modes* of order could be indifferent to the hierarchies around which order has rallied historically and that it seeks to reproduce?

Rather than homogeneously expressible, the calls for order and the doling out of punishment that are so prominent in our time would seem only to reinforce the old geopolitical maps eager, since colonial times, to establish the unequal distribution of roles that the reproduction of capitalism demands as its *sine qua non* in different countries. Not losing sight of that colonial inheritance means, among other things, that far from constituting the evidence that critical thought need only verify, the forms that the "authoritarian turn" of neoliberal capitalism adopts across different geographies present a challenge for theoretical, analytical efforts to thematize them.[2] Conversely, under the current conditions of foreign submission – whether financial, judicial, cultural, or military – imposed by some nations over others, to generalize a negative judgment on appeals to national sovereignty in the name of freedom and a more impartial justice would entail omitting one of the dimensions of inequality against which many emancipatory projects are currently struggling. Would it be possible to think the political potential of the "national question," as it were, "untethered" or abstracted from the "colonial question" and the geopolitical asymmetries that continue in its wake? This exercise in abstraction, would it not persist in a colonial mode by de-problematizing the national question as a *question*, and by presupposing as a valid principle the meaning that appeals to the nation carry in the core countries?

The reading hypothesis that I seek to explore in this chapter takes on the arguments developed in chapter 1 and interrogates them in the context of figures of the nation and the emergence of new nationalisms at an international scale. I have argued that the authoritarian neoliberalism exploited and encouraged by the Alianza Cambiemos, which was in power in Argentina during the period from 2015 to 2019, figured the community as simultaneously a community of punishment and sacrifice. As participants in a "cultural revolution" that supposedly put an end to a decade of decadence, we should have recognized ourselves – according to Macri's government's interpellation – as subjects infinitely guilty of holding on to false expectations about rights owed to us, and we ought to have been willing to participate in all manner of sacrifices to purge that fault. But, simultaneously, we ought to have recognized ourselves as morally superior subjects and implacable executioners upholding a judgment without trial over others who refuse to submit. The argument that I have gestured at, and that I now want to develop, is that the rhetoric of Macrismo did not limit itself to applying this dialectic between aggression and submission on an internal plane, but projected it also on the international plane, making room simultaneously for expressions of xenophobia *and* the undermining of national sovereignty, in a gesture that differentiates it both from the new nationalisms emerging in many countries, as well as from previous neoliberalisms in Argentina.

From the Picaresque to Joyful Sadomasochism

As I pointed out in the previous chapter, the dominant social humor in Argentina prior to the coming to power of Macri demanded simultaneously more (negative) freedom and more control; less "anarchy" and less "authoritarianism"; the opening of a "dialogue" scrubbed clean of all political conflict; the reinstatement of order, of hierarchies that egalitarianism had erased; and systems of reward and punishment that, according to the majority's perspective, had been ignored. This ideology, more or less unconscious and affectively charged, expressed itself through exasperated denunciations of "anarchy," supposedly fomented by social policies that were "indifferent" to personal effort, and in diatribes against political measures oriented toward establishing reference prices for financial markets and a market of goods in favor of consumers – measures that were, nonetheless, seen as "authoritarian" regulative gestures of a political power intent on interfering with individuals' daily lives. This increasingly central sensibility, interweaved in narratives of personal self-sufficiency, revealed a fear of "others" who were under- or over-represented but always suspiciously threatening, as well as an emphasis on "punitive security" and familial relations, figured as the only possible guarantors of peace.[3]

The most authoritarian aspects of this constellation of disciplinarian anxieties and punitive, harmonistic, and deregulatory desires were rehearsed and fostered by policies championed by the government between 2015 and 2019, as well as by the discourse of its functionaries. Those policies included the decision to suppress the law that sought to limit the monopolization of media companies, as well as the decision to decrease levies on grain and mineral exports in order to benefit the more privileged sectors of the economy. But among those policies it is worth highlighting the fact that the government gave the military permission to intervene on issues of internal security, through a presidential decree that went against a stable consensus upheld by different democratic governments since the end of the last civil–military dictatorship in Argentina, an agreement that established a necessary distinction between acts of defense and acts of security.[4] Complementing this measure, adopted in the guise of fighting drug trafficking, in the name of freedom of circulation and the population's being "fed up" with street blocks and "insecurity," the government also sought to impose: a "protocol of conduct" in public manifestations that essentially allowed for the violent intervention of security forces in social protests; a "no occupation" protocol against student protests in secondary schools in Buenos Aires; a change in the regulations on the use of weapons by security forces that permitted them greater firepower; the modification of the national law on migration to the detriment of migrants' human rights through a decree of necessity and urgency (DNU) that was ultimately found to be unconstitutional; and the creation of a detention center for migrants. According to the section dealing with migration in the 2017 report produced by the Centro de Estudios Legales y Sociales (CELS, Center for Legal and Social Studies), where it discusses the state of human rights in Argentina, the DNU number 70/2017 by which the executive office sought to modify the previous norm involved a turn in migration policy from protection to criminalization, and "enabled the deployment of a tool of social control with vast consequences for the processes of naturalization of migrant persons, in particular those of limited resources," by attempting to entrust migration processes to migratory authorities, in coordination with judicial authorities and police across the various jurisdictions.[5]

These policies were accompanied by numerous statements by members of the government who backed the intervention of police, gendarmerie, and naval power in cases of so-called "*gatillo fácil*" ("easy trigger"); who justified "taking justice into one's own hands" on the part of civilians facing cases of "insecurity"; who vindicated the carrying of arms for "legitimate defense" to petty crimes and, simultaneously, identified as "terrorist" practices the acts of protest organized in the south of the country by the Mapuche community.[6] The endorsement of racism and xenophobia, which reached fever pitch in the declarations of Patricia Bullrich, the minister of security, on the subject of the aforementioned protests, was also evident in the widespread suspicion on the part of functionaries regarding the rates of delinquency among foreigners, deemed to be higher than among nationals; in their complaints that foreigners were using public hospitals; or in their requests that public national universities declare the number of non-Argentines taking courses for free in them, as well as their chosen majors.

All of these policies and public displays on the part of functionaries from Macri's government can be understood, in a way, as part of a securitarian, punitive turn, which is not new in Argentinian society, and which, as Gabriela Seghezzo and Nicolás Dallorso pointed out, has been consolidated in subjectivities since the mid-1990s and articulated through social relations by the spread of individualizing fears, and distrust toward popular sectors and foreigners, as well as toward state capacity and even politics itself as the frame that could mediate social problems.[7] But if throughout the course of Carlos Menem's neoliberal government (1989–99), this punitive securitarianism was associated with incentives for private consumption and a market-mediated leisure that paired well with the ironic, hedonistic style of the former president, and with a cynical attitude that did not hesitate to point out the interested particularism of all subjective practice, Macrismo exalted, conversely, as I have pointed out, the superiority of the morality of austerity, discipline, and submission. Its diffusion of a xenophobic punitivism, which included but went beyond the amplification of securitarian logics and pre-existing policies of repression, also brought out a certain nobility in suffering and coalesced a new ethos of sacrifice (of the self) and punishment (of others) that not only worked on isolated individuals but also enveloped the nation as a whole: the nation, too, had faults to atone for.

In essence, in a move that could be seen as contradictory with respect to the perpetual fanning of old social prejudices against foreigners, Macrismo's (self-)punitive rigorism was not radical only when it came time to make the individual responsible for their fate, but also denigrated a national culture that had "raised us to be vagrants and quick to find shortcuts," making it difficult for us to recognize that effort *as such* constitutes a superior moral value, and that "there's nothing more important in a person's life than the dignity that comes from one's own work." In particular, the "*viveza criolla*" – a supposed Argentine aptitude to develop tricks that allow the individual to gain advantage even at the expense of others – was at the receiving end of severe moral condemnation on the part of Macri,[8] in direct contrast with the exaltation of this same "cunning" in Menem's neoliberal picaresque, which tended to celebrate it as a gift. Indeed, the cynicism of Menem's neoliberalism represented an exacerbation of particular interest that thrived in underlining its own interested particularism and that vindicated without any ethical nuance the art of the sneaky deal which was nonetheless a useful means to get ahead and secure one's survival, whereas Macrismo's neoliberal discourse renounced even the instrumental rationality of self-conservation, declaring effort, discipline, and the disposition to submission as superior moral goods, independently of all goals – as if ethics required an irrational, limitless adherence to authority and its religious lexica of purifying effort.

Voicing such negative judgments on national cultural features that marked our spiritual difference from "serious countries" was certainly not new: these views were held both by the liberal oligarchic governments of the end of the 19th century and the start of the 20th century and by the neoliberal governments that preceded Macri. But Macrismo seems to have gone deeper in its desire to re-establish our "honorable" identity of "humble" providers of raw materials and debtors on the international scene – a submissive quality that was only implicit in the slogan "Argentina, granary of the world" championed by the old patricians; in the exasperated nationalist discourse of the last civil–military dictatorship; or in the supposed egalitarianism of the exchange rate parity and the unrestricted openness to importations spearheaded by Menem's government.

During the 1990s, Menem bragged about his "post-nationalism" and his willingness to be a docile player in the world order, taking on whatever position this order had in store for him. The subordination that his government proposed was not immune, however, to a hedonistic overtone, spliced with images of forbidden pleasures, which was synthetized in a phrase of the then minister of foreign relations, Guido di Tella, referring to the foreign policy the country would follow. In a moment when the world seemed to promise interconnections, consumer novelties, and multiculturalism ushered in by the fantasy of a friction-free, borderless capitalism, it was a question, in di Tella's terms, of "sustaining carnal relations" with the United States. Mauricio Macri's attitude on July 9, 2016, during the celebration of the 200th anniversary of independence from Spain – which incidentally coincided with a visit from the former King of Spain Juan Carlos I – made clear, on the contrary, that submission had to be seen, in the best of cases, as a pleasure in itself. In a speech that featured prominently the heir to the crown that once owned us, standing next to him and addressing him, the former president of Argentina said: "I am here trying to think and feel what they [the people who declared independence] felt in that moment. Clearly, they must have felt anguished in their decision, dear king, to separate from Spain." The punitive, sacrificial neoliberalism of Macri's government represented the only neoliberal neocolonialism that was still possible when the more "enlightened" side of that ideology had entered into crisis.

Between Submission and Fauna: Neocolonialism and De-Historicization

The privatized, hierarchical, and culturally conservative ethos that, according to Wendy Brown,[9] allows neoliberalism to represent the nation as a home in need of protection and that is a fertile soil for the growth of xenophobic, misogynist, punitivist political formations not only has permeated neoliberal sensibilities in Argentina since 2008, but was also characteristic of Macrismo's discursive universe. However, its rhetoric lacked the rousing, self-aggrandizing quality of nationalist ideologies in the core countries; in its stead emerged a call for submission and sacrifice that, without ceasing to fan the flames of a selective xenophobia, did not stop preaching that the "fault lies with Argentines."[10] As I have been suggesting throughout this chapter, this highlights a difference between the authoritarian overtones of Macri's government and existing nationalisms in other regions,[11] as well as the hedonic, ironic neoliberalism that preceded it in Argentina. But we still need to delve deeper into our understanding of the diverse strategies at play in the political spread of an authoritarian neoliberalism.

In the Right represented by Macri, it was possible to discern a confluence of multiple, diverse senses of "familial privatization," with which neoliberal ideology knows how to pair economic privatization. If Macrismo was privatizing from the point of view of ideology – and not only in an economic sense – this was not only because it rehearsed and enabled conservative values already present in society. Macri's administration indeed exhibited and reclaimed – above all through the pronouncements of some of its functionaries, among them Patricia Bullrich and the former vice-president Gabriela Michetti – strong attachments to the classic identitarian topoi of traditional Argentinian historiography with which the country's patricians historically demanded submission and sought to discipline the population: from the so-called "Conquest of the Desert" to the exaltation of a rural, simple, humble life, all the way through an unconditional support for the armed forces.[12] However, at the same time, Macrismo also insisted on erasing history through a gesture of simple and plain de-historicization.

On the one hand, the symbols of traditional authority were reinstated, and it was demanded of us that we reconcile with those institutions charged with perpetuating the asymmetries and violence that marked the founding of the nation-state. In a brutal gesture, neoliberal discursivity situated itself "beyond" the problematizations that the nation's dominant history had been subjected to due to persistent social mobilization. On the other hand, however, Macrismo abated the most profound disinterest in anything remotely historical, which was then displaced *in toto* as the province of artifice and corruption. The practices of Macri's government were privatizing, in this second sense, because they managed to impose from the start a political style forged around the idea of "proximity" that allowed it to fashion itself as the only non-political political force, situated "beyond" ideologies and the struggle over historical symbols, including national names, languages, and emblems. But due to this same centrality of the idea of proximity, the erasure of history and conflict in the government's rhetoric did not operate – as it did during the neoliberalism of the 1990s – through a technocratic appeal to expert, neutral knowledge that would be placed *above* all partisanship. Macrismo endeavored to erase history and conflict through the constant mobilization of domestic, ego-centered passions, which libidinally reinvested the language of social administration and which, in official rhetoric, was situated *below* or in the paradisal *anteroom* of artifice and divisions that would later on become politics and history.

In other words, with the ascendance of Macrismo's familialization, we not only have the *appearance* of a patrician history consecrated by the dominant tradition, but we also have the simultaneous *disappearance* of history as the possibility of transformation. Everything that was violent but also contingent in history was substituted for a history always identical with itself, whether we are talking about the eternal whales that the government imprinted on bills (replacing national heroes)[13] or about parental love. The omnipresence of fauna and familial relations was certainly a way to conceal emancipatory struggles, while the canonical icons of the establishment and reproduction of order likewise tended to disappear. Along the infinite proliferation of images of a nature supposedly self-identical, originary, immediate, this ideology wished to leave behind, once and for all, history's divisions and contingency, in order to leap into the eternal: me, my pet, my children, my neighbor.

In this leap toward eternity, the national question was ushered off the scene. If nationalism constitutes a mechanism to flatten the wrinkles of the national question by turning it into an unproblematic identitarian mark, the government of Alianza Cambiemos managed a similar effect by evaporating it along with history and moving to the terrain of nature, a space that it was hard-pressed to leave except when an authority figure visited the country: the King of Spain, representatives from the Sociedad Rural Argentina (Rural Society of Argentina), the International Monetary Fund, or the president of the United States. Coming face to face with these figures, the sacrificial, disciplinarian component of this ideology adopted the submissive position that has been bestowed upon it by History. Conversely, when it is a matter of a *history* that, raising the national *question*, emerges as unresolved and demands an interrogation over a pending justice claim, the natural kingdom and homely passions returned to the center of the scene in order to displace history and thus the national question evaporated alongside it.

In agreement with Wendy Brown, we could say that neoliberalism effectively tends to make the nation into a political non-problem, into a home insufficiently guarded. However, in the case of Argentine neoliberalism, it would be necessary to add that this phrase should be understood in terms of a two-pronged political strategy. On the one hand, it is the strategy to reinstate neocolonial logics that have been historically dominant and that demand the submission of the national population in the world order. On the other hand, it is the occlusion of all the instances in the nation's history that are indices of an irresolute past, which are designated as extensions of a self-identical nature. Using different language, we might say that Argentine Macrismo taught us that a punitive, familial discipline did not have to be self-aggrandizing or hold imperialist aspirations and that it could, in turn, manifest itself in two different modes (without being incompatible): as a (self-)punitivism that, due to the central idea of sacrifice, reinstates old hierarchies inside the nation while it is willing to assume a neocolonial submissive position with respect to the "greats" in the world order; and as a politics of symbolic "subtraction" that, by erasing from the historical space the conflict over interests and values, effectively enables – much like the former mode – a timeless morality, untethered from sociohistorical conditions in the formulation or realization of its precepts.

The fact is that the experience of this type of political Right confirms an old intuition of many popular movements in Latin America. That is, that the consumption of ready-made national identities – emptied of all complexity, excess, and internal discontinuities – is not emancipatory; nor is the framing of the national question across the region to be seen as the end of all identitarian unease with respect to one's own participation in the social fabric; nor finally – precisely because of the aforementioned – are all forms of "overcoming" the national question to be seen as desirable. In what other way but the national question could we raise here and now urgent topics such as, for instance, the rights of the Mapuche or the Qom in the nation-state; or the State's responsibility for growing malnutrition, unemployment, and indebtedness in the country; or the legal proceedings for crimes against humanity committed in the national territory during the last civil–military dictatorship by the repressive forces of the nation-state? It is through the national question that we have, not infrequently, come to experience what Walter Benjamin would claim is history's pain and failure.[14] And also what has yet to be redeemed.

7

Dialectic of the University

The image of a dialogue between the university and society and the question over the possibility of critical thought are historically connected. If dialogue evokes the idea of communication between them, it also demands the presupposition that the university is autonomous and can thereby, precisely because it is not to be identified with society in its current state, sustain a reflexive, critical relation with respect to society. During the 19th and 20th centuries, however, the tradition of critical thought persisted in interrogating that which, in the figures of dialogue and intellectual autonomy, remained ideological, as pretense or obfuscation of thought vis-à-vis its effective social and historical conditioning. From a materialist tradition more or less close to Marx, but that is still willing to inherit Nietzsche in a distinctive way, both the image of a peaceful, unrestricted social functionalization of the university and the assumption of its imperviousness with respect to society came to be the objects of ideology critique: the former because it demanded adjustment to what is socially current, enthroning the status quo as the insurmountable horizon of thought and social practice; the latter because it perpetuated the idea of an Absolute Spirit, safely distant with respect to the vicissitudes of the world and immune to its crises.

In our own present, an index of the ideological character of this confidence (in the autonomy of knowledge) is found in the insistence on the *question* of the university, its critical potential and limits, in a moment of crisis and punitive reformulation of neoliberal capitalism. This interrogation, which we develop mostly in university spaces, is itself affected by history – both at the level of the question itself and at the level of what the question means or what it puts into play. If today we are asking about the possibility of a dialogue between the university and society, what is at stake is not only the "communicational" problem of how to carry forward a critical outlook produced by the university to society in a moment of crisis, but, above all, the conditions through which this critical outlook could come to be. We ask about the university because its existence as a critical institution has ceased to be evident, yet, nonetheless, critiquing the present seems necessary. The question of the critical university emerges, then, in a determinate moment, a critical moment (a moment of crisis) in which it seems more urgent than ever not only to resist the dominant social, political tendencies but also to counter-propose, likewise from the university, forms of novel praxis to them. But if critical practice is understood not only as thinking *about* a given state of the world but also as the emerging practice *of* that state, its immunity is no longer guaranteed. So we come to the paradoxical status that haunts every critical practice alert to the historical developments that create it: whereas a kind of thought that fancies itself immune to the present crisis would necessarily reproduce the illusion of independence of Spirit that characterized idealism, conversely, by knowing itself affected by the situation in which it seeks to intervene critically, it could not assure itself of its right to existence (or existence itself).[1]

In this chapter, I intend to uphold the idea that, for critical thought today, it is not evident that there is an autonomous university left to defend and, simultaneously, that we cannot assume this supposedly radical realism to be the endpoint of our analysis. If the crisis of trust in the existence of critical thought in our academic institutions is far from being a pure loss, the disillusioned diagnosis of the sheer functionality of the university in the social landscape in which it is found should be followed by a consideration of the academic institution that is willing to examine its internal tensions: that is, the coexistence in the institution itself of practices that do not cohere with, and even contradict, the neoliberalization of life that is pervasive in today's world. A university that is unable to think its participation in social reproduction *and* social transformation could hardly foster the formation of critical thought, regardless of how elaborate and immanently informed its research findings are. The issue is how a university that does do some of that would deserve to be understood. Or, in other words, the question is whether we will be thinking more critically if we recognize the contemporary university as a monolithic neoliberal device, or whether it is not more productive to treat it as an object that is not identical with itself and where political conflict is immanent. It is this last kind of approach that, following Adorno, one might call dialectical, understanding the dialectic as a critical modulation oriented to "[dissolving] the rigidity of the temporally and spatially fixed object into a field of tension of the possible and the real."[2]

Universities and Neoliberalism

In Argentina, even though the figure of the "entrepreneur" has become central only relatively recently, the spread of market values throughout the university was given a strong boost by the "opening to the world" and the application of neoliberal economic measures during the Carlos Menem presidencies (1989–99).[3] During the 1990s, the technocratic legitimation of implemented policies and the imposition of efficiency and competitivity indicators as paradigms for the rational distribution of resources managed to enthrone economic rationality as the only valid criterion by which to judge extra-economic practices, including the production of knowledge. Through the application, at the national level, of international standards of evaluation of researchers and of the "quality" of higher education around those years, both the university system and research institutions were strongly reconfigured in accordance with the productivity demands of a new academic market. The language of "human capital and resources" came to replace references to "students," "teachers," and "intellectuals"; there was a greater concern with the number of mentions and citations of publications, and a diminished emphasis on the content of research or its capacity to generate debates *in* and beyond "academia"; and, at the subjective level, it became evident that the disinterested search for knowledge (supposedly required by modernity) lost ground to the demand for the management of careers on the part of teacher-scholars whose academic success or failure came to be openly judged in the entrepreneurial lexicon: constant investment of personal effort without guarantees of stability and with significant risk; the proactive utilization of opportunities; networking, competitiveness, and achievement indicators.

Such symptoms of the widespread imperative for self-valorization in the university reached new heights in the country after 2015, with the explicit endorsement of entrepreneurship on the part of Macri's government (2015–19), and became further intermingled with the anti-intellectual currents latent in Macri's familial version of neoliberalism. As I argued in chapter 2, even though it can be readily tied to active policies of de-legitimation and even prosecution of subjects and institutions associated with "the intellectual," this anti-intellectualism also transcends those policies. This anti-intellectualism configured itself as a two-sided emotional, social disposition: a readiness, on the one hand, to understand as *threatening* the reflexive efforts that insist on the non-self-evidentiality of the reigning social reality and the opacity of one's own subjective desire, and, on the other hand, to experience as *liberatory* those gestures that aim to prove the transparency and simplicity of immediate reality.

In its more repressive, persecutorial aspects, at the level of political mobilizations, the self-proclaimed "cultural revolution" of Macrismo did not stop at cutting – as Menemismo also did – the budgets of free public universities and the funds for national research in science and technology while insisting on self-financing, but also actively delegitimated intellectuals, researchers, teachers, and the public university itself. This was a political gesture that, in turn, promoted and gave expression to a more or less diffused social anti-intellectualism, which became manifest in, for instance, the harassment of academic institutions spearheaded by the dominant media, but also the "*escraches espontáneos*" (spontaneous public shaming) of teachers and researchers in social sciences and humanities across social media.[4]

However, the foregoing impression given of a university threatened from the outside by entrepreneurial, anti-intellectual logics would not be particularly trustworthy. As several texts have shown, both in the region and in the world at large, market rationality and an anti-intellectual disposition have influenced, from the inside, the institutions and practices of knowledge production since the end of the last century.[5] If punitive neoliberalism endorsed dispensing with a reflexivity that it postulates as superfluous, in the university itself self-reflexivity about its own practices – generally broached by theoretical investigations – has long come to be suspicious, even when that suspicion has been sometimes voiced by appealing to the paradoxical argument that since theory is omnipresent, it does not need a properly institutional home. The affirmation – confident that we have left positivism behind in the advancement of science – that every empirical investigation implies the application of concepts often led and continues to lead to the conclusion that the theoretical developments necessary for the production of specific knowledge have already become available or should be the province of each area of specialization. Beyond enshrining the fragmentation of knowledge, what is problematic about the assumption that each discipline, or even each research project, must apply its own concepts to achieve its particular "objectives" is that it tends to naturalize research goals by excluding a broader question: what kind of society produces these goals as knowledge objectives in the first place? This renders superfluous the existence of theoretical investigation dedicated to what used to be called critical theory of society. Thus, this diagnosis leads not only to the practical banishing of any reflection that cannot demonstrate its immediate use for applied research, but it also gives airtime, from within universities themselves, to arguments that legitimate neoliberal educational policies which, from outside the university, demand, plan, and administer the incessant reduction of theoretical research, as well as any totalizing reflection interested in the study of the complex, often inconspicuous mediations involved in the production and reproduction of social cohesion.

The Argentine Free Public University: Estrangement or Radical Critique?

From the point of view of a critical theory of knowledge proposed by Adorno, we could say that even if such a harmony between the university common sense and what is socially dominant is not intentional, this matters less as exculpation of universities than as the index of the massive presence *in* them – and despite their claims of autonomy – of that anti-intellectualism that, precisely, would be one of the tasks of science to conceptualize with the purpose of facilitating a transformation of both knowledge and society. So, if, on the one hand, in the face of the stigmatization of which the university is the object, it is more or less clear that we need to actively defend the university in general, and, in particular, the free public university that demands rights, institutions, and experiences of knowledge under threat, on the other hand, it is necessary to emphasize that the defense of the "autonomy" of the university such as it currently is could be paradoxically in sympathy with its de-differentiation from the social landscape in which it participates. It is a prohibitive defense – as the ambivalent French term *defendre* luminously suggests – that entails making peace with the plainest common sense prominent in these supposed "cloisters" instead of demanding of them that they stand, as a social force, against the privatizing neoliberal securitarianism, by keeping open a zone of inquiry where neither the world nor the human is treated as self-evident.

When compared to a radical critique of the university, the specificity of Adorno's argument lies in the fact that while affirming the ideological character of the university's so-called "autonomy," it does not arrive at the conclusion that we are dealing with a consummate heteronomy or even at a diagnosis of total homogeneity. The point of elaborating a critical theory of contemporary society as it relates to the production of knowledge would lie, according to Adorno, not so much in confirming that this autonomy is false or that it has simply ceased to exist, but rather in enabling a reflection about the dimensions of heteronomy that affect knowledge as such in order to highlight the partially pending character of this autonomy and demand its effective realization.[6] So, whereas a radical critique of knowledge would tend to see the actually existing university as a coherent instrument of power *instead of* a practice associated with the production of truth, for the Adornian argument the critical procedure is dialectical and produces the estrangement of available identities. In other words, it consists not in the substitution of one identity for the other, but rather in the dissolution of a rigid identity of the object in order to deploy it as a field of tensions that the object, as object, renders invisible by presenting itself as a coherently structured, undivided unity.

In his book *Filosofía (y) política de la universidad*, Eduardo Rinesi performs a similar dialectical reading of the free public university in Argentina, even though he certainly does not appeal to the term "dialectical."[7] If in that book, the contemporary university emerges as a set of practices that neoliberalism has (re)modeled – for instance by turning it into a career services hub, where isolated individuals compete among each other for professional opportunities – the reality of the university is also figured as being in excess of that neoliberal identity. The Argentine free public university, Rinesi claims, in tune with the arguments of Willy Thayer[8] and Sheila Slaughter and Gary Rhoades[9] about the neoliberalization of higher education and the international academy, has had difficulty thinking through the heteronomy that shapes it. This heteronomy comes not only from the ostensible "outside," the Market or the State – which during the last neoliberal government effectively deployed an aggressive policy of promulgating entrepreneurship in the university – but also from within, insofar as it has docilely adapted parameters (of efficiency, productivity, competitiveness) and in general the market morality imposed by neoliberalism as the criteria to measure value across all practices, including the production of knowledge.[10] However, referring specifically to the Argentine situation, Rinesi emphasizes, on the one hand, that state policies during the last several decades came into conflict with what Slaughter and Rhoades would call the capitalist academic regime of knowledge and teaching, and, on the other hand, that acknowledging the determining weight of that "immanent heteronomy" is particularly urgent when it comes to institutions where research is disconnected from teaching (even more so than in the free and public national universities). This is due to the fact that, in the 1990s, research institutions in Argentina took on more quickly and efficiently than public universities the imposition of quantitative evaluative metrics, which came to displace the question about the social relevance of the produced knowledge. But it is also because, during the governments of Néstor Kirchner (2003–7) and Cristina Fernández de Kirchner (2007–15), scientific research revealed itself to be more insular and reluctant to problematize its neoliberalization than public universities.

Effectively, in a conjuncture defined by a set of public policies promoted by the Kirchner governments – among which we count the creation of several public free universities across the country,[11] budget increases for universities and research and development in science and technology, and the embrace of the Declaration of Cartagena in 2008, which held that the university is a public and a social good, a universal human right, and a responsibility of states – Argentine public universities could give space to a debate about their social relevance that had hitherto taken place only in the margins, mainly due to the insistence of critical journals and magazines such as *El Ojo Mocho*, *Confines*, and *El río sin orillas*. That debate entailed an interrogation of what universities produce, how they do it, and what their relation to society should be. This debate made palpable the tension between the metrics of academic performance and the social question of who was entitled by right to study in a free public university – as well as the question over the institutional structures required to secure this right – and made the common features that universities had predominantly acquired as they implemented neoliberal policies into a problem of public concern.

Precisely because they proved themselves capable of confronting an unresolved tension between supposedly immanent demands that in reality commodified the logic of research and broader social demands that came into conflict with that logic, public universities revealed themselves to be a terrain of struggle and not quite a space thoroughly entrenched in the demands of neoliberalism. They emerged, in other words, as a field immanently divided, able to generate a certain logic of costlessness that did not square with the market parameters that also defined them and that, as a political excess related to the right to education, was not incidentally less legible where research was dissociated from teaching.

The ambivalence that defines this image of the university is not due fundamentally to the preventable logical contradictions of a deficient interpretation, nor to a dose of optimism that would want to compensate for an overly pessimistic diagnosis. This ambivalence is a product, rather, of a certain dialectical perseverance that advises us to remain alert to the sinuous internal structure of complex institutions – or at any rate is more complex than a categorical account would suggest. Not without contradictory dynamics, these institutions have been able to sustain, in Argentina, a critique of their own current constitution as well as of the imperatives that rule them, and they have insisted, at the same time, on the responsibility that falls on public universities to construct a more democratic sociability.

Among the efforts that bear witness to the responsibility of producing democratizing, socially relevant work, we find: social science and humanities research that, working in tandem with human rights movements, has highlighted the pending nature of justice and the enduring damage of the crimes against humanity perpetrated by the last civil–military dictatorship; works in the arts that persist in elaborating a collective memory while experimenting with novel ways to represent experiences of collective suffering during that dictatorship; work on the role that communication studies played in reconceptualizing communication as a social power that could not be administered by media monopolies under strict market logic; and, finally, the insistence on the part of all these disciplines to regard education as a social right whose existence must be collectively guaranteed, and not left to the vagaries of the market or to the unequal self-managing capacities of individual students.

All of these socially relevant interventions on the part of the public university helped to problematize the crystallized social senses of justice, memory, communication, and education, and they did so by shaking up the assumption that these terms are self-evident, estranging them from their usual meaning, and demanding a rethinking of them, in order to make their usual meaning less restrictive, limited, and unjust. These interventions deserve a reading that not only is attuned to their past appearances but also perpetually demands comparable socially relevant interventions from the university. These interventions, which enliven the university and reveal its internal complexity, do not come out of nowhere. Such vitality on the part of the university was no stranger to, in the Argentine case, the open potential created by a broader sociopolitical context that, while making visible the value of knowledge for the whole of society and for democracy,[12] favored the deployment of a reflexive process within the academy, as well as a deferral of the question over the "utility" of knowledge toward the problem of its "social relevance." It has done this even when the main political forces operating in the current context have not formulated these effects as their goals, which suggests that neither the university nor the broader political context coincides fully with the more or less coherent identities it projects.

This framing manages to de-absolutize the image of the university as a sheer neoliberal construct (an image that many critiques of the neoliberalization of the university have entertained), and does justice to the internal complexity of the Argentine free public university. A radical critique of the university has the undoubted virtue of correcting the academicist abstraction that encouraged us to trust in the self-assured criticism of knowledge. But its own gesture tends to become abstract when it turns trust (scientism) into fatalism (biopolitics), and assumes as the endpoint of a critical interrogation of the "social determination of knowledge" the diagnosis of a consummate heteronomization, or rather the untenability of a pretense of autonomy. Today it is no doubt necessary to distrust the confidence in an already given autonomy, but it is also necessary to insist on the fact that autonomy, understood as the critical power to question the present, is not only a blanket illusion, but also the very thing under threat by cultural logics propelled at a global scale by a punitive, anti-intellectual neoliberalism. In the Argentine university, which has been neoliberalized during the last few decades, not everything is neoliberalism, and it is precisely against that excess that in several countries across the continent various anti-intellectual tendencies – promoted by an ideology that has left behind the multicultural utopia and today openly flirts with authoritarianism – have positioned themselves.

The University and the Critique of the Present

Despite facing increasing social resistance that sometimes manages to politically consolidate into opposition against neoliberalism, both at the regional and at the global level we are witnessing not only the spread of the logic of market self-valorization as the sole parameter of merit and just distribution of resources, but also the spread of a militant anti-intellectualism that pathologizes any reflexive effort and seeks to impose the inexorability of current inequalities. Giving this political-ideological conjuncture, it is not enough to say that there is no autonomy in knowledge because our academic institutions reproduce heteronomy from the inside, letting themselves be overwritten by market logics, nor is it enough to claim that it is imperative to defend the autonomy of the university against the attacks of the new right-wing movements that threaten it "from the outside." Rather than uncritically assuming that autonomy of knowledge actually exists or denouncing its current impossibility, questioning the potential and limits of academic institutions to produce critical thinking about the present would seem to require the *simultaneous* presence of two clashing theses: on the one hand, that there "is" no autonomous knowledge to defend; and, on the other hand, that it is imperative to defend the autonomy to which knowledge should aspire. The first suggests that we cannot expect a decisive intervention without sustaining a critical reflection on the current neoliberal reality of the university. Rather than as the last bastion of resistance to dominant tendencies "outside," these institutions must be thought of as spaces where these tendencies are actively reproduced, whether under the guise of researchers' "entrepreneurship" or in the fantasy of the independence and neutrality of effective knowledge. On the other hand, however, the new punitive inflections of neoliberalism, determining the specific configuration of new right-wing movements worldwide, demand of us that we defend the autonomy of the university, its right to exist as a complex institution imbricated in various, even contradictory, ways in the social web of which it is a part.

Democracy requires autonomous institutions and practices, an autonomy that should not be confused with self-sufficiency, but rather is the capacity for reflection about the multiple ways in which we depend on others and how our decisions and practices affect them in turn. For knowledge, this means that the best odds in the battle against anti-intellectualism lie less in the university's capacity for self-preservation, and more in its capacity to continuously question its own social determination and relevance: that is, its own self-awareness as a social force, affected by social modes and dominant tendencies in society, and willing to intervene in them. A "socially relevant" knowledge is not necessarily a "useful" knowledge, not necessarily because it is "not useful," but because it relates critically to what, in a given moment, appear to be the unsurmountable limits of the political and social imagination. And it relates critically to those limits not by doing away with them, but by situating them, that is, by anchoring them in specific conditions whose mutability and emancipatory potential it likewise highlights.

This negative, reflexive potential is socially relevant today not only in the sense of enabling a critical, potential expansion of the social horizons structured by neoliberal governments, but also in the sense that it favors "non-securitarian" modes of dealing with contingency given the growing precarity and vulnerability associated with the contemporary development of a globalized financial capitalism. As Pablo Oyarzún remarks,[13] if the securitarianism fomented by a punitive neoliberalism is associated with the instrumental side of the enlightened project of knowledge (we know to be safe, to acquire a certain power over those who cause fear), the potential for reflection, which emphasizes the artificial and thus contingent character of the established order, elucidates the limits of the fantasy of total control over existence. This fantasy necessarily reproduces fear as synonymous with life while attempting to "once and for all" be rid of fear by eliminating its supposedly "evident" causes. The move of dissolving this evidence as evidence could well be one of the key tasks at a time when precarity only seems to grow at an increasing rate, thus accentuating the securitarian tendencies in our societies.

But this move to dissolve what is evident can only emerge from a situated movement. The social relevance of the negative, critical potential of knowledge depends on its ability to take note of its place in its own context, and to make an effort to read this context in all its complexity, not as a consummate horizon, but as a field of forces in tension. The point is to propose once again the problem of autonomy *as a problem*; of encouraging the porosity of our own academic institutions; of reading them internally as battlefields and not as homogeneous blocs. But above all, it is imperative to read them as social forces: surfaces on which deeply consequential social and political disputes continue apace.

8
Spectrology of the Right[1]

What Remains

By the time someone reads these words, Macrismo will have left us with an outrageous foreign debt, a devastating social debt, and also a lexical debt, with words exhausted by their flattening in the diet of the government's prose. It will be time to take stock, to ask about what remains, time to determine, with as much precision as possible, what it is we are up against. Then, it will be urgent to remember that taking stock of the damage done should not make us lose sight of the emancipatory energies that managed to make their way among so much destruction, energies that are quite possibly necessary to keep pushing our era beyond the ignominious immanence of an eternal present that neoliberal capitalism inhabits and makes us inhabit. Among what we have inherited from this ominous epoch will be not only material and symbolic debts, but also collective potentials more or less recently revealed against the will of the times. These potentials constitute a real force not always recognized or easily identifiable in a reading of history. However, any materialism or realism that does not give up on the popular aspiration to happiness and justice, and that moreover resists the empiricist vertigo toward literality and complete facts, will have to reckon with these potentials. It is not enough to limit oneself to the account of deficits; one must also persist patiently in the art of spectrology, namely, in the interrogation, wherever they emerge, of unresolved forces that strive for a less cruel world and disparage the present as normalizing and overly complacent to the demands of a post-utopian capitalism.

The future government will inherit *that*, too: that which does not add up to a calculable set of managed goods, and that consists rather in a series of collective movements that are shaking up the region today. It will inherit, among other things, the insistent force of "feminisms"; of the workers' movements and the movements for human rights; of students in Chile, Argentina, and Brazil; of indigenous groups in Ecuador and Bolivia. These are malleable forces and not at all predictable in their tactics – much like those of the leader of Kirchnerism – which sometimes overflow into hitherto uncharted terrain and shake up our sense of what political gestures are possible. Could it not be them, alongside the unions and social movements that knew how to mobilize during those ominous years of humiliation, that could beckon the effective implementation of that "neoliberalism, never again" invoked by Cristina Fernández de Kirchner in her speech on October 17, 2019?

Rather than "remaining," in the sense of being bequeathed from generation to generation as cultural property, similar forces "rest" in history precisely because they do not, because they resemble ghosts that cannot find peace and return again and again whispering nightmarishly in the brain of the living, as tokens of the damage but also of the possibility of redemption. Until it erupts as popular rebellion, this whispering is, for the most part, undecipherable, not a recognizable maxim or refrain that could withstand unaffected the passing of time. One must not ask what is left of revolution – Horacio González once wrote in an extraordinary text recently recovered[2] – because revolution is not a model that one can copy more or less well. Revolution is only what comes through in shreds; what "rests" by refusing to rest. It is the partial and displaced remainder that in turn displaces the present where injustice persists. Such are the concerns of spectrology: the thought of a stunted, imperfect inheritance, of a sleepless remainder, and of the secret covenant across generations, which obsessed and obsesses those who refuse to stop reflecting on the chances of an emancipatory politics, from Marx to Derrida, by way of Walter Benjamin and Auguste Blanqui.

But specters, as we know, are not only those of emancipation. For whoever is reading these words, Macrismo, or rather the right-wing politics that has claimed its name, will *not* have *left us*. That Right, which was neither particularly democratic nor particularly new but still managed to disorient the political scientist, which has left us – once again – with so many disasters in the economy, imagination, and life, will still be here, among us, showing up to brandish the banners of security, vengeance, xenophobia, and explicit racism and classism. It would amount to a rationalist simplification and a political error to interpret the uninhibited expressions of explicit punitivism – by Carrió and Bullrich[3] – during the elections of 2019 in mere tactical terms, as aspiring to "consolidate the hardcore base of Cambiemos." Unlike multicultural neoliberalism, the punitive kind has succeeded in thrashing the promissory dimension of its predecessor and yet has managed to stimulate several specters that already exhibit good health and are disquietingly resonant in a society where, as much as we regret saying it, it is not at all clear just how prevalent emancipatory or egalitarian desires really are.

We need spectral analysis – which can bring into focus the power of ideologies, myths, and desires that are operative today precisely because it resists the overly neat distinction between absences and presences – *also* to think through the persistence, subsistence, and enabling of the Argentine Right. That spectral analysis is not only vital to evaluate the potential for an emancipated life, but is also necessary to conceptualize that which indefinitely *defers* it or simply *prohibits* it. This emphasis on negativity is, no doubt, the crux of ideology critique. But the "negativity" attributed to it is not necessarily opposed to an emphasis on the emergent subversive imagination; these are only opposed when this negativity becomes abstract. But in fact, there is no interpretation of the emancipatory potential that can simply leave untouched issues such as powerlessness and reactionary, resigned, or desperately defensive behaviors. To think concretely about the new subjectivities implies thinking through the obstacle presented by the here and now, and, as part of its fabric, the real force of the calls by those who announced a "cultural revolution" just yesterday, thereby indefinitely casting out the promise of social justice. These are the calls organized by the re-encounter of sensibilities that will no longer tolerate "the people who don't know how to vote," or who "live on the backs of the industrious middle class," or who "are like monkeys, eating each other's lice."[4]

Did we read those calls correctly? Who could or can answer them? How much denial of the authoritarianism latent in this neoliberal capitalism is hiding behind the economistic explanation for the decline in votes for Macrismo? We would do well to try to understand in phantasmagoric terms these gestures proper to a homegrown Right that plenty of political analysts prefer to ignore or to interpret soothingly in instrumental terms, because they are much more dangerous than an electoral tactic and are not properly described in terms of purely defensive moves. The work of these gestures consists actually in nothing less than bringing to the world, to invoke, or to revamp again the specters of right-wing life.

Right Reloaded

Since (at least) *The Terminator* (James Cameron, 1984), the dystopian, futuristic movies that characterize the post-multiculturalist neoliberal capitalism of our time have always displayed a moment where "power," the system, matrix, or network – seemingly as invisible as it is invincible – that was on the verge of dying in the previous movie, is revamped at a new and higher level. This is the moment called "recharged" or "reloaded" and that implies not a simple return, but an infinite potential of "evil," fantasized as incommensurable or simply unlimited. In politics, however, we know that "evil" is unlimited only in the image of omnipotence that it seeks to project; in the tremulous representation of its suffering victims; or in the idealist political philosophy it evokes, whether in its Platonic, Heideggerian, or biopolitical versions.[5] Beyond these instances – which are effective and extremely real as imaginary configurations – we know that, just as there is no "Power" (fearful corruptor of virginal beings in the figurations of the beautiful soul or in anarchism), the Right never acts as an abstract evil or something unlimited. It is rather a question of a specific production of harms unequally distributed in a rather precise way, which is directed, however, by a force with a dispersed presence: transversal and varied in intensity across the entirety of the social fabric that this force seeks to transform fundamentally at the level of sensibility and the social unconscious.

The ubiquity of right-wing life (to invoke Silvia Schwarzböck's expression[6]) contrasts sharply with the strict, unequal localization of harms, and therefore the Right cannot be thought of as a finite set, coherent and stable, with consistently determinate boundaries. We also know that it cannot be something that starts and ends with changes in government, nor is its fate to be dictated simply by electoral defeats and victories. Such is the limit of the idea of a cultural battle when it suggests the image of politics as requiring entry to a field where two opposing stable identities are in conflict, which – thanks to the "correlation of forces" – culminates in a determinate political situation, fixed until the "battle" starts once again.[7] The Althusserian idea of critique as continuous breaks – which also seeks to correct the abstraction of a metaphysical evil while resisting its replication – is, by contrast, more precise: rather than great cultural battles enrobed in the symbolism of epic drama, the transformation of ideologies is shown to be a work of excavation that must be constantly renewed, appealing to modes and terms that must be continuously reinterrogated and that lack the kind of horizons of reception fully prefigured in advance.[8]

That idea of critique as a continuous break involves an anti-narcotic effect: it alerts us to the fact that the ideological Right can be reloaded even when electorally defeated. Neither a metaphysical evil that persists in the depths despite appearances, indifferent to the other political forces, nor thinkable in the terms of the limited time spans of the electoral calendar – as in, for instance, what emerged victorious over the cultural politics of Kirchnerism and predictably became sharper with the coming to office of Cambiemos, only to be defeated at the ballot this year [2019]. None of this is totally unfathomable, but if between ideology and one's vote there are certainly complex relations, there is never identity, just as there isn't identity between the temporality of ideologies and the orderly segmentation of time into four-year periods.

This applies to the recent past, as it does to the near future. Cambiemos, in 2015, reinterpreted and gave expression to a pre-existing social Right whose existence it encouraged from political office not only through repressive acts on the streets, but also fundamentally through the spread of the sacrificial spirit in the plundered masses and the promulgation of self-repression as synonymous with dignity. The administration's cultural program aimed at hyper-responsibilizing the individual, who was forced to learn that their luck depended on their own constitution and to plumb the depths of their interiority for the causes of their unhappiness and current powerlessness. The program of a cruel neoliberalism did not promote – as Menem's technocratic, globalizing neoliberalism did – consumption or a cynical skepticism about values, but rather asceticism, conventionalism, and faith in the harshest forms of self-discipline. That was its promise of salvation: "You can die of starvation, but as long as your body burns in rising flames, your soul will be saved from the joyous corruption which marked your life until now." This was the promise that the government broadcast while it multiplied the number of entrepreneurial programs and courses of "Ontological Coaching" that – as we saw in the previous chapter – graced the websites of the "illustrious" (free, public, massive) University of Buenos Aires and the scientific CONICET.[9]

Today [2019], in Argentina, a reloaded Right is, at a strictly political level, what explicitly encourages the country's Bolsonarization and is ready to fight for it, invoking specters. It is the Right who can suggest or explicitly claim that blond is beautiful; that what's poor is brown and what's brown is idle; that idleness is inherited and a sort of spiritual syphilis that is prevalent below and is necessary to extirpate by the root. It is the Right who says that we must have a new "Conquest of the Desert"[10]; that the slums must be detonated; that we must live in uncertainty and enjoy it; that the poor are to blame for their fate, and must seek forgiveness in the Church for complaining instead of humbly accepting their allotted place in God's kingdom. These are not outbursts, mistakes, or lapses. And neither are these mere electoral tactics to consolidate the (alleged) 32% of voters. Both the economicist reading of the results of the primary elections in 2019 – not incidentally the one that the dominant media subscribed to – and the one coming from the experts in political engineering – which exhausts the power of fears spurred by stigmatizing discourses in immediate results – obstruct our understanding of the meaning of the "cultural revolution" announced by Cambiemos in 2015, as well as its afterlife. Such an understanding is of the utmost urgency. That is because it is around this inconclusive, and thus pending, promise of transformation of the national spirit that the specter of right-wing life is constituted today, a specter that will continue to haunt us in the years to come.

Cultural Revolution and Authoritarian Sensibilities

Is it possible – as has been done before – to interpret the content of that revolution as a "never again populism" or a "never again Peronism"? If we don't, we run the risk of being abstract since it is precisely in opposition to these forces that the political movement in question tends to identify itself. But, conversely, we can only conceive of the movement in this way by resisting the temptation to fetishize, which would seem to not need interpretation, and keeping in mind that, given its high degree of mutability, those names – far from self-evident – are not enough to describe what would be in danger if the "revolution" comes to be; a particularly pressing danger when the ghost does not care to pass in silence the authoritarian lineage that even in 2015 it tried to disavow.

Multiple and superimposed are the planes and temporalities of the ghostly constitution of "insecurity" – which justifies the generalized carrying of arms and happy triggers; of the myth of the "wily" migrant who has come to "plunder" our public services in education and health; and of the "idle, parasitic welfare mom" ("*planera mamá luchona*") – guilty *a priori* and without chance of salvation since she would have been equally guilty if she had wanted an abortion. All of these objects of hatred, diffused by the "cultural revolution" and reiterated in everyday conversation, do not emerge in a single administration, nor are they exclusively caused by that administration's cultural politics. Nor is the subjectivity capable of sustaining them easily formed in four years. We therefore need to expand the interpretive frame in such a way that, in the specificities of the political field in Argentina, one can still hear not only the resonances of what neoliberalism produces at a world scale, but also the ideological productivity of capitalism, as it has emerged transformed following the crisis of the postwar democratic pact. In this sense, the "cultural revolution" of Cambiemos is not self-made, nor is it limited to censuring certain impulses of the population. This revolution exploits rather, as well as multiplies, the subjective fears generated by the constant threat of being jettisoned by the system that produces capitalism in its neoliberal phase. It says: given that there is not enough for everyone, find your own parasite and eliminate it. But in doing so it does not only encourage us to offload great quantities of aggression latent in our relations with others, it furthermore frees us from the sensation of powerlessness vis-à-vis a mode of social organization that systematically undermines all possibility of real subjective autonomy.

Therein lies the hypnotic appeal of the slogan "*¡Sí, se puede!*" ("Yes, we can!"). When during the campaign of 2019 Mauricio Macri rehearsed this slogan *ad nauseum*, he was referring no doubt to the possibility of reverting the results of the 2019 primary elections, but at an ideological level he fundamentally sought to cancel yet again all modicum of subjective mistrust about the unrestrained self-responsibilizing imperative projected by neoliberal capitalism in its sacrificial, punitive inflection. This capitalism only recognizes subjects who are as omnipotent as they are guilty. Unlike others who had to accept it as a human right, for this capitalism, "social justice" is an oxymoron – because everything trans- or superindividual is essentially authoritarian and constitutively unjust – a mere legitimation of vagrancy, or equivalent to demagogic corruption. In the imaginary enabled by the so-called "cultural revolution," the term "security" has lost all its vestigial associations with the welfare state – which persisted in that arcane construct "social security" – and of the social rights owed to citizens; whereas "freedom" amounts to the infinite capacity to adapt and indeed the obligation to do so, at whatever cost and independently of what the odds are of achieving one's goal ("Doing what needs to be done"). Effort is actually more noble to the extent that it is irrational. Thus, social de-responsibilization for the fate of the individual and hyper-responsibilization of the latter to the point where they are not even limited by the rationality of the impulse for self-preservation are two key pieces of the new morality that the apparatuses of the "cultural revolution" are intent on broadcasting and even enacting in their own rituals.

But only in a radical constructivism or through the hypothesis of a full subjective destitution that is the correlative to the real subsumption of life under capital are these discourses, imaginaries, and *dispositifs* translated immediately in the subjective realm into an insensible lived experience which is paradoxically incapable of *any* experience. Only through this frame of intelligibility is the subject fully and coherently "constructed" or something already immunized for the tensions that, borne by the I, in previous moments made them into a problematic and potentially problematizing instantiation. By contrast, from the point of view of the concept of ideology, which implies in diverse ways a certain inconsistency in the order and a certain distance from it that one aims to measure – a distance that not infrequently sunk the concept itself, whether in an illusion of literality or in idealism – there are always reservations about the hypothesis of total consummation. This prevents ideology critique, even while considering the efficacy of mechanisms and the polished finish of their effects, from losing sight of the fact that we are dealing with a developing process, which is, to an extent, reversible; a process that never deals with pure bodies and *dispositifs*, and whose result is an experience more or less damaged rather than impossible. For ideology critique, the subject, as product, is always also a mystery, a question mark, an instance to which one must pose the question: what will you do with what has been done to you, or, rather, what is in it for you?

The domain of ideology critiques is not that of the no-longer-subjects (incapable of experiences) or of those full subjects (in the sense of identical to the *dispositifs* or mechanisms that interpellate them). Nor is it the domain of individualities that miraculously continue to be free in a world that no longer or not yet is. Its concern is spectral analysis. Not only in the realm of doctrines, rituals, and slogans, but also in the realm of social sensibilities that organize the more or less typical modes of processing the former. How long does it take to configure the sensibilities that constitute the substratum of conscious ideologies, those desires only vaguely intuited by their carriers, those inexplicable preferences? In what ways are they configured? What are some of the fault lines undermining those formations? These are the very concerns of ideology critique conceived as spectral analysis.

In a famous text about Brechtian theater, Walter Benjamin held that it was not a matter of asking what was the position of this or that artistic movement *with respect to* the dominant mode of production but of investigating how it was *in* the mode of production; it was a question of style.[11] If we understand the latter as the mode(s) to inhabit a dominant experience, the ideology critique of the "cultural revolution" of the Right could be thought and practiced, in a realm different from the analysis of political discourse, as a stylistics: an interpretation and mapping of the state of subjectivity in a scenario where the dominant vectors are social de-responsibilization, hyper-responsibilization of the individual, precarization of life, and growing inequalities. How are they situated? In what way are subjects today disposed *in* that field of forces? Which are the possibilities that are enabled, and which are prohibited by those subjective styles? Is the despised particularism of the cynic and their cunning attitude still the privileged mode to process experiences of injustice? For how many people is that relatively relaxed illusion of detachment under conditions of increasing precarity still available? To what extent does the experience of oneself as waste, the radicalization of the sensation on the part of the subject of their absolute dispensability, contribute to desperate attachments – more rigid, authoritarian, and cruel than the typical attachments from the 1990s in Argentina? Would it be more promising to conceive of a style that, unlike the previous ones, is perpetually, emotionally moved by the ills of the world but turns up its nose at any organization or concrete action in the struggle against those ills, rendering the link between that emotion and a collective transformative practice "unbearable"? To what extent might this anti-political moralism actually be constitutive of subjectivities that, in other respects, we might otherwise consider open to an ethical interrogation of the other and of others in the here and now? To go on rehearsing answers to these questions would probably help us to imagine perspectives of the right-wing "cultural revolution" with greater precision than the scientific study of political engineering. In that study of style – even more than in the varied electoral results – could lie the key to what we are up against.

9

Chainsaw Capitalism

The Milei Moment[1]

> Not utopia but a realistic struggle to grab the bone from the other dog – that is our program. Not peace but incessant struggle for survival; not abundance but the lion's share of scarcity. Can you realistically expect more?
>
> Leo Lowenthal and Norbert Guterman, *Prophets of Deceit*[2]

In December 2023, Javier Milei became president of Argentina, thereby inaugurating a far-right government that, in its search for the creation of an unrepressed capitalism, in just a few months annihilated salaried workers' purchasing power; set legal precedents for the newfound emphasis on the primary sector of the national economy ("re-primarization"); cut the budget for public education and health care; partially or fully dismantled several institutions tasked with fighting discrimination, as well as policies crucial for the memorialization efforts related to the crimes against humanity perpetrated during the last dictatorship (1976–83); claimed to have brought about "*el mayor ajuste en la historia de la humanidad*" ("the largest cuts in the history of humanity")[3]; and effectively repressed social protests while preserving considerable levels of favorability. The global attention that the rhetoric and incendiary policies of Milei's government have garnered constitutes one of the indices of the extreme character – even in the context of a generalized rise of right-wing extremism – of the positions held in Argentina by the current administration, which fashions itself "libertarian." From the critical-ideological perspective I have been pursuing in this book, however, it is just as important to avoid the normalization of this kind of phenomenon as it is to resist the feeling of awe vis-à-vis its presumed exoticism.

Mileism is far from a lightning bolt in a clear sky. Both understanding its ideological conditions of possibility and interpreting the singular inflections it introduces to the broader context of rising right-wing movements across the world are crucial critical tasks today. But it is not clear we have the necessary categories to carry those tasks forward. When I began this book, I suspected that the concepts forged around the "nineties" image of "postmodern" subjects, wavering between technocracy and cynicism, were not sufficient to give an account of the intensely moralizing, punitive, and sacrificial re-politicization that was becoming prominent after the financial global crisis of neoliberalism in 2008. Likewise, today it is reasonable to raise doubts about whether the concept of a moralizing, order-obsessed neoliberalism is sufficient to critically interpret political identifications organized around a euphoric absence of limits, and political interpellations that fancy themselves anti-systemic and take disinhibition to be the expression of, if not synonymous with, freedom.

We find once again that the prevailing concepts to think through the former neoliberalism are not enough. And yet, given that there is no such thing as the reading of a conjuncture that is radically dissociated from concepts, and no transformative action that remains on the margins of a reading of the here and now of our action, it is necessary once again, from both a theoretical and a political point of view, to attempt conceptualizations to name this present moment. What concepts should we privilege, then, to bring to light the most distinctive features of the "Milei experiment" and to name the mechanisms upon which its efficacy depends? Would it be timely to speak of "post-fascism," "right-wing populism," or "authoritarian neoliberalism"? Or rather, faced with this case, would it be more "enlightening" to use the image of an "anarcho-capitalist utopia"? What are the terms that are capable of encapsulating its singularity without losing sight of the role that both long-lasting local processes and contemporary global tendencies played in its emergence?

The focus on these two dimensions, for which I initially use the terms "local" and "global," organizes the critical interpretation of Mileism that I offer in this chapter. In order to give an account of the singularity of the phenomenon, in the first section I attempt a reading of the changes that the Milei interpellation introduces in the kind of expectations and formulas encouraged by the neoliberal Right that preceded him: namely, the neoliberal Right led in Argentina by the former president Mauricio Macri (2015–19), whose model of subjectivity, at once self-sacrificing, meritocratic, and punitive, constituted the central object of inquiry of this book. My reading hypothesis holds that Milei's interpellation undoes the relatively tense combination that existed in the Macrista ideology between, on the one hand, enabling individuals to exercise cruelty upon others deemed weak, and, on the other hand, appealing to "a return to order" and peaceful retreat into domesticity. Milei undoes this knot by encouraging an unencumbered affirmation of the right to exercise violence on others in the public sphere. Moreover, and fundamentally, he displaces the promise of a "return to order" so that the violence unleashed upon others is no longer codified as a disciplining that recovers lost hierarchies, but rather takes on an emancipatory sheen. To put it succinctly, according to this neoliberalism, which styles itself as "libertarian" – the repression of social protests notwithstanding – "the chaos" and the "perfect storms" are not to be fought in the name of order, but should instead be interpreted as the manifestation *of* and the condition *for* "freedom," which, in turn, is understood negatively as deregulation and the disinhibition of passions for property and unlimited capital accumulation.[4]

But what are the historical conditions in which this speech can *take hold*?[5] I argue that the rise of Milei is unthinkable without the figuration of a limitless, de-historicized subject that was actively encouraged by former president Macri between 2015 and 2019. Yet at the same time, I posit that part of the novelty of Mileism lies in its capacity to exploit a post-apocalyptic sensibility, only partially configured before the COVID-19 pandemic, and which by 2023 it was no longer possible to satisfy with promises of an anti-conflictual, familial, securitarian character that had been initially promoted by Macrismo. Under the Milei dispensation, the authoritarian content of right-wing denialist, repressive, and anti-egalitarian policies has become explicit.[6]

Nonetheless, in this new "post-apocalyptic" version of the Right, these old policies seek their consistency in the subjective realm following a logic of public agitation and exhibition of destructive passions, rather than calling for a silent, resigned withdrawal into private life. The subject to whom Milei spoke during the electoral campaign was not a subject that was confident in their self-sufficiency, but a resentful subject, who felt that their power had been usurped and actively sought revenge. From the perspective of this subject, the more dysregulated the dynamics of social exchange, the greater the chances to eliminate the supposed "privileges" awarded to others in the form of social rights. However, they would also have more opportunities to prove themselves a "lion" – along with the chainsaw, the central figure in the iconography broadcast by the current government – who is capable of prevailing in the chaos.

Now, as is obvious for those of us who have paid attention to current trends in international politics, neither the existence of a resentful subject, nor the politics of affects deployed in Argentina by Javier Milei are exclusively local phenomena. In a certain sense, this libertarian, anti-establishment discourse could be interpreted as a particularly shrill case of the same conservative agitation that characterizes contemporary authoritarianisms. They affirm the ineluctability of capitalism, only this time not under the silent banner of a resigned, quotidian personal adjustment, but under the explosive form of an authoritarian freedom where the other can be unabashedly described as a mere parasite who, insofar as they present an obstacle to the development of the I, must be eliminated. However, while holding that the consideration of the historical conditions of possibility of this genre of phenomena exceeds an analysis in terms of national history, it does not necessarily imply that we must ignore the uneven impact that an openly predatory capitalism – free from the limitations of the postwar democratic pact – has on the so-called "center" and "periphery" of the world. Therefore, in the second section of this chapter, taking as points of departure two icons of the contemporary Right – the wall and the chainsaw – I examine the asymmetrical geographies of an anti-democratic tendency that is "global" yet not immune to the uneven character of the "globe," not to mention an enduring colonialism. One may suspect that, without being exclusively Argentine, the most emphatically thanatic modality that the affective exploitation of social frustrations acquires in Mileism distinguishes it from other agitational discourses that are rampant in what is usually known as the "global North" – discourses which are mostly configured around the conservative image of a presumed collective identity threatened from the outside and whose integrity it is necessary to protect.

To put it in a formula: Milei is not Macri, but neither is he Trump. If the *temporality* of an overdetermined series of crises that mined the credibility of an entrepreneurial "*¡Sí se puede!*" ("Yes we can!") separates him from Macri, the unequal structure of a "global" space that – in spite of the promises of "unlimited circulation" – continues to be marked by a strict division of international labor and financial indebtedness separates Milei from Trump. This does not mean that it is possible or desirable to think these ideological-political formations in isolation or through the logic of a straightforward external comparison. If a materialist theory attuned to the Hegelian "perspective of totality" can no longer content itself with thinking differences as simple expressions of identity, it cannot ignore either the authoritarian, presentist nucleus that links Milei with Macri and Trump in a moment when the "normal" reproduction of capitalism seems to depend, at the ideological level, on the proliferation of imaginaries that systematically construct whole sectors of the society as parasitical and eradicable.

I contend that delving deeper into this "systematic" relation between the various authoritarian imaginaries and the reproduction of capitalism constitutes the dialectical excess that a critical materialism can illuminate, in opposition to a descriptivism that is as positivistic in the epistemological realm as it is resigned in the political one. And it is precisely because it refuses to concede to the logic of consummated facts, presumably incomprehensible, that Max Horkheimer's famous warning seems to me as true today as it was in 1939 when he first uttered it: "[W]hoever is not willing to talk about capitalism should also keep quiet about fascism."[7] Moreover, I think that in order to earn the adjective "critical," this analysis should also undertake a critique of the language in which the critique is formulated. Hence the quotation marks around terms such as "global," "local," "global South," and "global North." Would it be possible and desirable to take for granted the critical sense of this language? Or should a critical theory sensitive to existing regional asymmetries historicize this language in light of situated conjunctures, in order to prevent those same "critical" terms from reproducing the geopolitical and economic inequality they were meant to denounce?

Faithful to the skepticism of naturalized "progressive" concepts voiced by Walter Benjamin in a famous letter to Horkheimer,[8] but also faithful to a Latin American tradition of essayists according to whom it is not possible to think through a problem without turning the very language in which we discuss it into a problem in turn, in the last section of this chapter I return to the "categorial" question – already hinted at in our introduction. I propose, by way of a corollary, a critical reflection about the language of critical theory and, in particular, about the resonances of the term "global" in the Latin American critical landscape. It is possible that this term, so familiar in contemporary thought and that certainly seems difficult to replace, might not be up to the task of thinking "the concept of history" that a critique of the present demands, and that it is our task to produce.

Political Responses to the Crisis of Neoliberal Capitalism: From Order to Disinhibition

In *How Will Capitalism End?*, Wolfgang Streeck proposed a characterization of contemporary capitalism that linked the crisis of the accumulation model prevalent after the 1970s to social apathy and political regression. In contrast to the hegemonic aspirations upheld in earlier moments, Streeck argues, in this new phase of post-hegemonic capitalism, the dominant classes gave up on the idea of founding a just society, limiting themselves instead to "founding *social integration* on *collective resignation* as the last remaining pillar of the capitalist social order, or disorder."[9] This gave rise to the emergence of a decadent capitalism from beyond the grave, which in turn was expressed in a generalized "under-institutionalized way of life" and an "under-governed society."[10]

Streeck's emphasis on apathy and collective resignation as central characteristics of the prevalent social affectivity in 2016 – when the book was initially published – strikes us as strange in the context of the authoritarian politicization that in Argentina and beyond, already at the start of the century, was rather more closely associated with public displays of a growing and increasingly agitated social malaise.[11] But his hypothesis interests me because it allows us to introduce certain relevant terms for the discussion of the political proposal Milei embodies today. Is it possible to describe it as an exponent of the abdication of the goal of founding a more just society on the part of the dominant classes? And if so, would it be a mere "withdrawal" from ideological disputes that would simply leave the field open for the slow return of a pre-institutional, pre-political violence? Or are we facing a political-ideological phenomenon that is actively produced and amounts to a break with a fairly generalized presentism? Is it timely to characterize Mileism as an effect of resignation or of a conservative vocation? Or, at the opposite extreme of the political spectrum as far as subjective experiences of historic time are concerned, should we think of it instead as a revamping of utopian thought, as a genre of radical, even anarchic, "utopia," in striking contrast not only with "presentist" apathy but also with a moralizing restoration?

As the point of departure for the retrospective exercise which is necessary to begin answering these questions, we should note that one of the novelties of the political campaigns that preceded the 2023 elections in Argentina was the emergence of right-wing proposals – among which we found Milei's – that explicitly addressed the crisis of neoliberalism and proposed strategies to combat it, starting from the premise that the prior inflection – optimistic, multiculturalist, globalist, entrepreneurial, and even "progressive" – had entered its terminal phase, and that neoliberal policies would need to be revamped in new terms. Certainly, we are not dealing with a radical break. Building on previous interpellations, these proposals idealized a typical neoliberal subjectivity for which what is at the root of life and progress is personal effort, grounded in a power we all naturally have by virtue of being individuals. Appealing to the traditional terms of this doctrine, these new proposals continued to idealize the old self-sufficient subject of neoliberalism, for whom cooperation is only conceivable as a secondary byproduct of existence and not as the necessary condition of possibility for life as such.[12] However, what distinguished these novel inflections from other neoliberal discourses that remained prevalent in the electoral landscape was that they presupposed that this self-sufficiency was no longer immediately available for individuals, that it had been wrested from them, and that a new effort was needed to identify and suppress the so-called "usurpers."

In contrast with the optimism of the entrepreneurial formulas broadcast by Macrismo in 2015 – "*¡Sí se puede!*" ("Yes we can!"), "*¡Tu único límite lo ponés vos!*" ("The only limit is set by you!"), "*¡Si no lo hacés es porque no querés!*" ("If you don't do it, it's because you don't want to!") – but likewise in contrast with the anti-conflictual slogans of other candidates from Macri's party that participated in the primaries of 2023 – "*Ahora la tranquilidad*" ("Tranquility now")[13] – the campaign slogans of various exponents of the local Right sought to connect with an individual for whom the crisis had stopped seeming a fearful horizon and instead had become the absolute sign of the present. The individual whom they sought to interpellate certainly did not have trust in a progressive historical development, but neither did they find anything soothing about a resigned confirmation that history is finally nothing but the circular scenario where effort is perpetually needed. "*Se necesita fuerza para detener el caos*" ("Force is needed to stop the chaos")[14] and "*¡Viva la libertad carajo!*" ("Long live freedom, goddamnit!"),[15] the new slogans of the neoliberal Right post-crisis, spoke to an audience that experienced the present historical moment in dystopian terms, positioning themselves simultaneously beyond progressive optimism and resignation in the face of the eternally self-same. That audience could no longer readily think of themselves as carriers of an unlimited power because, from their perspective, the catastrophe had already happened, and they were less worried about the rights they might lose than about the thievery of which they felt themselves to be the victims. Its pathos was expressive of a new post-apocalyptic social sensibility that, beyond all confidence, experiences what exists as a massive, unambiguous degradation.[16]

This new post-apocalyptic social sensibility that had germinated in light of successive economic crises, political crises, and the health crisis provoked by the COVID-19 pandemic clearly marked not only the proposals but above all the particular tone of the discourse deployed in the electoral campaign of 2023 by both Milei and the candidate for the then opposition party, Juntos (formerly Cambiemos), Patricia Bullrich. In an active political interpretation of these subjective conditions and deploying the deeply subjectivizing and shaming mechanism that Macri had already used, these interpellations exploited the idea that the Peronist administrations had definitively turned Argentina into a "cradle for paupers"[17] and turned to placing blame on alleged culprits responsible for the generalized powerlessness experienced by the individual. To do so, they appealed to a host of strongly discriminatory social stereotypes that were not new – the welfare beneficiary, the protestor, the public employee, the unions, the feminist movement, politicians in general, and Peronists in particular – while ignoring the broadly structural inequality of Argentine society, or attributing those structural injustices to systematic "interventions" of some malign spirit: the "*casta*,"[18] the State, or the various "collectivisms" in Milei's parlance. In any case, these discourses embodied what could be described as a neoliberal revanchist active politicization that centered on the existence of harm, the actuality of the crisis, and demanded a drastic, courageous political intervention to address it.

However, within the frame shared with other right-wing political forces, Milei's central and decisive particularity lies in the fact that his intervention displaced the order/chaos axis toward the repression/freedom axis. And thus, rather than addressing the self-perceived status holders, promising to restore the status they had supposedly lost, he oriented himself toward those who did not have an imagined "glorious past" to which to return. Instead of referring to the lack of order or the degradation of old hierarchies, as early as 2019, Milei's discourse landed on a critique of "repression" and of what he called "privileges," thereby endowing his speech with an emancipatory, plebeian tone. This tone was reinforced by his public image, a street-smart scenography, and the disorderly, tumultuous atmosphere of his public appearances as candidate. Whereas some of his political adversaries insisted on reclaiming "force" to discipline a "chaotic" society, in Milei's speech the existence of repression as such emerged as part of the problem rather than the adequate mechanism for its resolution. The answer did not lie, according to Milei, in a return to order, but in the emancipation of market energies following the example of "free countries":

> The countries that are free grow twice as much as countries that are repressed. [. . .] The poorest have double the income of those from

> the repressed country. [. . .] It is better to be the smallest dog in a free country than a big shot in a repressed country. [. . .] Besides, in the free countries, poverty is 25 times lower and people live longer than in a repressed country. What sustains this virtuous cycle? The five basic institutions of capitalism.[19]

As would become explicit in the talk at Davos that President Milei gave on January 17, 2024, for him, however, "collectivism" is extremely widespread, and also includes those nations that in 2019 he called "free countries." Even those countries need to be "freed" from the "repression" afflicting those people who are ashamed when someone "tells them their ambition is immoral."[20] Thus the self-proclaimed "lion" pretends to stand as the only world leader truly bringing about the end of moral inhibitions and the only representative of the forces of "freedom" against "repression," in a sort of global capitalist pseudo-utopia that will give rise to a "full capitalism," unprecedented in the history of humanity.[21] In any event, his discourse was always structured around the dichotomy freedom/repression in terms of slogans as well as in his public appearances. As time went on, these became increasingly violent. It was no longer enough to verbally thrash "repressed countries" in TED Talks and TV studios. It became necessary to create scenarios in which disinhibition could be performed. So, by 2023, while his adversaries endeavored to *stop* chaos, Milei's political acts seemed brazen in the face of crisis and even attempted to aestheticize the violent destruction of the status quo, as if the efficacy of its interpellation depended on the construction of a climate of euphoria *in* and *for* chaos, figured in interminable explosions, demolitions, collapses, and radical shearing with a chainsaw in hand.[22]

In the context of a political arena where the major forces in Argentina assumed the insuperability of capitalism, the call to a final disinhibition of repressed market energies formulated by Milei distinguished itself, in no small measure, because it managed to make of capitalism an event, and a pseudo-emancipatory event at that. Refusing to promise calm, more management, or the reinstatement of order by force, Milei managed to reinvest market social relations with the allure of radical novelty, and thus turned himself into the Messiah who had come to redress the theft of energy that the State, the *casta*, and collectivism had committed against individuals. With Milei's intervention in the political conjuncture, the apparently unquestionable datum of our epoch – capitalism – became a promise of a new beginning, and thus a solution to the crisis of neoliberalism presented itself: one that was "expansive" and "agitated" and that turned out to be more electorally viable than the other reactionary, neoliberal answers on offer.

Agitation without Utopia, Anti-Intellectualism, and Affective Exploitation

The turn away from the order/chaos axis toward that of repression/freedom, and Milei's staging of capitalism as a novel event during the Argentine elections of 2023, evinced immense ideological productivity, insofar as it was a solution to a local crisis of neoliberalism, and, moreover, made the sheen of the musty conservatism expounded by the other right-wing political forces in contention seem dull in comparison. Associated with the critique of "privileged strata," this ideological drift allowed, furthermore, for the political expression of deeply held class resentments proper to a mobilized society like Argentina's. However, far from projecting a "utopian" horizon understood as the partial anticipation of "what is not currently available,"[23] the noisy mise-en-scène of anti-systemic gestures on the part of Milei was and continues to be fundamentally *presentist* in the sense that it fulfills the function proper to contemporary authoritarianisms: to interpellate conservative capitalist subjects, incapable of imagining a kind of relation between people and with nature that is *not* structured in the terms dictated by unlimited capital accumulation.

In effect, from the critical-ideological perspective I have entertained in this book, those authoritarianisms not only acquire some of their conditions of possibility in the limits that capitalist social relations impose on democracy, but also generate political and subjective conditions that are necessary for the reproduction of capitalism. In that sense, their common main feature, as archaic or eventful as they might seem, is their active collusion with *contemporaneity*, their willingness to adapt to what is predominant in the epoch. Therein the problem with ideas such as neo*feudalism* and *anarcho*capitalism that are sometimes used to conceptualize these contemporary authoritarianisms. Rather than suggesting that what's at stake is a sort of pre-modern regression or a "libertarian" practice that defies *all* juridical norms, we should remember that, for example, slavery and other regimes of servitude are not prior to capitalism but a constitutive part of its globalizing process.[24] So we would likewise need to insist on the fact that as long as private property remains a principle immune to questioning or undermining, then it is not appropriate to speak of "anarchy." "Revanchist authoritarian neoliberalism" would be a more adequate term to name the present-day authoritarianisms, as long as we don't forget the *originally* anti-democratic character of neoliberalism in Latin America and, above all, that "there is no neoliberalism without capitalism."[25]

If we understand presentism as the eternalization of that which, in its own time, appears as the most current, we could say that Milei undertook a paradoxical presentist refounding through the production of a pseudo-event in which what was immediately given, the most contemporary, became absolutized, but also deprived of any semblance of internal heterogeneity. Rather than an aspiration to transcend the present, the idea of a "pure, unrepressed capitalism" – probably the only positive image that emerges in his discourse – works as a final universalization of the most "at hand" kind of relation one can conceive: the market relation. But beyond consecrating the present as an unsurpassable absolute in diachronic terms, presentism seeks to extirpate from itself and from the social fabric anything that, despite everything, continues to distort, de-totalize, and put stress on the more habitual modes of subjective experience: that is, a set of social, aesthetic, cognitive, and political experiences that often take their leave – even if partially – from the imperatives of capitalization, competition, and the exchange of commodities. In this sense, Milei's "pure capitalism" is presentist, too, because it wishes to be the end of those immanent dissonances that are latent in the social formations of contemporary capitalism. That is to say that his "pure capitalism" assumes not only the consummation of an *eternal* capitalism without the possibility of transcending it, but also the consecration of a *homogeneous* capitalist interiority, without dissonance, without signs of heterogeneous temporalities, without de-familiarizing imagination, and without complex processes immanently tensed that might disturb its purity.

Therein lies a second feature that Milei shares with other contemporary authoritarian formations and that has to do with the specific way in which these authoritarianisms reproduce themselves: its *anti-intellectual* tendency, understood not only as the censuring and persecuting of intellectuals – which it does – but also as a broader unwillingness to know: an emphatic, even euphoric, ignorance with respect to the social complexity and possibilities of transformation. In a synchronic plane, this militant anti-intellectualism would seem to express itself as a desire for unknowing the complexity of social life that renders unthematizable the more structural reasons for the widespread subjective malaise and that seeks to project isolated, relatively contingent elements as responsible for this. As the aforementioned speech from the closing of his campaign shows rather well, in Milei's case, that isolated, demonized element has generally tended to be "politics," postulated as the explosive cause of the ills experienced by the subject, and associated with corruption *tout court*:

> We have to expel the damn political *casta*. Let it be clear: this disaster that has taken place in the last hundred years did not come out of nowhere. It is not the fault of foreign powers, nor is it the fault of businessmen, nor is it the fault of honest Argentines, nor is it the fault of *el campo*;[26] it is the result purely and simply of politicians, who for the past few decades have ruled over us [. . .] with the sole purpose of making themselves rich at our expense.[27]

On the diachronic plane, this anti-intellectualism could be conceived as an attempt to de-historicize, a gesture through which processes are replaced by instants and the effects of a process of becoming emerge naturalized as if they constituted originary, insuperable facts. Whereas the apocalyptic sensibility we referred to above could be conceived as the false absolutization of a blatant catastrophe, and presentism could be the absolutization of the given, anti-intellectualism would seem to operate, by contrast, as a sacralization of the fragment and immediacy, manifesting itself as, among other things, the veneration of "pure facts," hypertrophied to a ridiculous extent in the pronouncements of Javier Milei, the "economist" and "professor."[28] As already suspected by Theodor Adorno when he referred to the techniques of fascist agitation in the 20th century, the "pseudo-concreteness" of the speeches by Trump or Milei does not necessarily come into tension with the abstraction that characterizes their slogans, but, rather, imaginatively compensates for the imprecision of their "gelatinous ideas" ("America," "Freedom"), leaving them, however, as indeterminate as before, and substituting argument with the accumulation of facts, especially numbers that are hard to fact-check, which invest the speaker with a special kind of authority.[29]

Finally, a third, related feature that Milei shares with most contemporary authoritarianisms in terms of the specific way they reproduce themselves has to do with the immediate, exalted form of managing social frustrations, fears, and hopes that Leo Lowenthal and Norbert Guterman encapsulated, in the 1940s, in the figure of the agitator. Unlike the reformer or the revolutionary leader, Lowenthal and Guterman argue, the agitator "works from within the audience, agitating what lies latent there." He does not seek to construct an objective correlative for his audience's dissatisfaction; he does not seek to elaborate on the social conditions at the root of social ills, but rather his speech is oriented toward "an aggravation of the emotion itself," giving his audience permission "to indulge in anticipatory fantasies in which they violently discharge those emotions against alleged enemies."[30] According to Lowenthal and Guterman, this affective exploitation works on the feeling of powerlessness that the individual has in capitalist societies, and closely allies itself with both anti-intellectualism – in the sense of giving up on investigating the processes and relations involved in the subjective malaise – and an apocalyptic sensibility, where discord and counter-tendencies haunting the present are erased.

But what would be the predominant affects that Milei's interpellation "aggravated"? As I suggested above, in this case, the affective exploitation seems to work on the popular resentment against alleged usurpers, but also a certain euphoria in catastrophe that Milei's party was careful to enable and aestheticize. In what specific ways and around which figures was this agitation made possible? We will turn to this question in the next section. But, to summarize, let's say for the moment that Mileism can, in effect, be thought of as a case of a presentist, anti-intellectual agitation that knows no utopia – a case which, as with many other contemporary authoritarianisms, naturalizes the effects of specific forms of the organization of life, ignores the long-term processes that produce those effects, and exploits the anxiety of the population in an authoritarian manner, proposing forms of violent, subjective re-empowerment that do nothing to ameliorate, and even worsen, the social conditions responsible for the malaise and sense of powerlessness.

However, the fact that Mileism shares with other contemporary authoritarianisms a series of conditions of possibility and a set of general mechanisms that guarantee the efficacy of its interpellation does not imply that it can be identified with them or that it can be criticized by appealing to the same categories. To critically interpret Mileism, we would need to ask, in Streeck's terms, whether there is actually, in Milei's interpellation, a pretense to found a just society, or, to put it in Adorno's terms, whether there exists in Mileism a promise and horizon of social reconciliation, or whether, more simply, something like an "order" in which collective life is possible is even imaginable. As we will see, to answer these questions in the affirmative is problematic. The militant anti-collectivism that characterizes Milei's discourse is less concerned with founding any kind of collective subject than with demolishing our current cultural narratives, not in order to bring about new ones but to emphasize a new cult-like relation between isolated individuals and objects of worship. Would we accept, then, to call Mileism "neo-fascism," "right-wing populism," or "restorative nationalism"?

Walls and Chainsaws: Toward a Critique of Borderless Authoritarianism

In South America the implementation of neoliberal economic policies in the 1970s went hand in hand with the coming to power of dictatorial governments.[31] Thus, it is somewhat problematic to speak "in general" of a neoliberalism that has become "punitive" or "authoritarian" only after the financial crisis of 2008, such as is proposed by certain periodizations of "neoliberal reason" fashioned after the European case, as, for instance, that of William Davies.[32] More to the point, if considered independently of the global mutations of capitalism, phenomena such as the South American dictatorships – which also include Alfredo Stroessner's in Paraguay (1954–89) and several regimes in Bolivia between 1964 and 1982 – are reduced to mere exotic phenomena. Therefore, as I have tried to show throughout this book, critical analysis should consider the web of global historical forces in which those phenomena emerge as possible and, in turn, the existing asymmetries between central and peripheric capitalisms.

As is widely acknowledged in the literature, during the 1970s Chile became the experimental laboratory of the economic policies that Margaret Thatcher and Ronald Reagan would "make global" a few years after – although cleansed of their dictatorial political form. With Pinochet's coup in 1973, in a remote corner of the planet, the world bore witness to the inaugural act of "neoliberalism," with which global capitalism announced its leave from the democratic pact of the postwar era, renounced its promises of integration, and lost the internal tension that, in the Keynesian models, had forced it to deal with the contradiction between the deepening of inequality and egalitarian policies. In contrast to that tense moment in capitalism, the neoliberal policies implemented particularly in the Southern Cone by all of the military dictatorships of the 1970s made it clear that there would not be room for everyone and that some would have to perish, whether by military hands or by those of the "world market."

As I have been arguing throughout this chapter, with the promised realization of an "unrepressed or unbridled capitalism" formulated by Javier Milei, South America would seem to be turning yet again into the trial run of a new experiment – an authoritarian economic, political, and ideological market experiment, which comes after the first great global crisis of neoliberal capitalism and constitutes its novel relaunching. Unlike what took place in the 1970s in South America, this experiment is taking place within the frame of formally democratic institutions. And unlike the neoliberal governments of the 1990s, it upholds a belligerent, abruptly sacrificial rhetoric rather than a hedonist, modernizing one. In the 2023 elections that brought him to the presidency, Javier Milei did not promise a "carnival of consumption" as the former – technocratic and neoliberal – president Carlos Menem did (1989–99). But, as we saw, he also did not promise tranquility and the restitution of social hierarchies. Instead he promised rebellion against what he called the "*casta*," which included not only the State and the political functionaries, but also all lawful salaried employees, whose income would be "*licuados*" (put in a blender, i.e. it would plummet).

As Cecilia Abdo Férez remarks, the pact that Milei sought to establish with his electorate was not premised on "the classic link between modern obligation of protection with security," but rather, on the contrary, associated "freedom with the increase of social insecurity, with the active production of social shelterlessness [*intemperie social*]."[33] His "unrepressed capitalism" did not promise unlimited circulation and consumption as counterparts to the adjustments that neoliberal policies demand from the population, and neither did it justify those adjustments with a call to the moral regeneration according to which our privations would redeem us from previous excessive joys. With Milei, the production of shelterlessness was proposed as itself joyous: it was no longer a matter of "painful sacrifices" that the individual must endure to expiate their guilt or to reach greater levels of consumption in a nearby future. Rather it was a sacrifice that would re-empower the individual when facing supposed usurpers by demonstrating a capacity to "cut" or "adjust" them too. Milei's symbol is the chainsaw, and in what follows I propose to interpret it as an index not only of the authoritarian response to the crisis of capitalism that haunts the globe, but also of the existing asymmetries in said "globe," which have been insufficiently remarked on even by a Frankfurt-style critical theory.

The point of departure for those powerful Frankfurt School critical analyses of 20th-century authoritarianisms was that these should be considered as "the wounds, the scars of a democracy that, to this day, has not yet lived up to its own concept."[34] This entailed rejecting the possibility of considering elements of authoritarianism as simply false and also voided the possibility of conceiving of authoritarian tendencies of the population as derived from individual psychic pathologies or as exponents of a pre-modern regression from the individual to the mass. According to Adorno, in the European fascist movements "true elements are also used in the service of an untrue ideology"[35] and the individual attachment to "fascist power" must be considered a perfectly modern response and, in a sense, rational when facing a situation where "the economic order, and to a great extent also the economic organization modeled upon it, now as then renders the majority of people dependent upon conditions beyond their control and thus maintains them in a state of political immaturity."[36]

In sympathy with Adorno's analysis, in the aforementioned study *Prophets of Deceit*, Leo Lowenthal and Norbert Guterman interpreted the social attachment to the speeches of fascist agitators in the United States during the 1940s as expressions of a subjective experience of powerlessness that had an objective basis, which the audience believed would be reversed through the purported new centrality conferred on the "little guy" in the fate of their country. Much like in *The Authoritarian Personality* Adorno had observed a link between "authoritarian submission" and "authoritarian aggression,"[37] for Lowenthal and Guterman what gave the speech of the North American agitator its consistency was the expectation of re-empowerment that his audience had and which he exploited without actually fulfilling it. In effect, even though the agitator promised his followers an active role in their liberation, in his eyes, the masses continued to be fundamentally passive: after the purge enabled by their mobilization, they would retire to their homes and leave government in the hands of the agitator. So, what was at stake in this particular kind of political mediation ("agitative") was, essentially, a false re-empowerment – not only due to the fact that the agitator's diagnoses of the causes of his audience's malaise left untouched and unsaid the systemic conditions that produced it, but also because it was an agitation that encouraged passivity, was depoliticizing, and was fundamentally conservative.

As we saw earlier, the call to mobilization against the "*casta*" formulated by Milei constitutes, in part, a particularly shrill case of this same "conservative [or presentist] agitation" analyzed by authors such as Adorno, Lowenthal, and Guterman in the last century. This kind of authoritarian re-politicization marks also many nationalist right-wing and far-right parties in the Northern hemisphere, under the loud sign of a false empowerment demanded by a group that sees itself as re-empowered at the expense of weaker members of society. However, a closer look at the concrete symbols brandished by parties such as Alternative für Deutschland (AfD) in Germany and movements such as Trumpism in the United States, on the one hand, and Mileism, on the other, could make us aware of certain geopolitical inequalities that are necessarily omitted in a generalized, abstract concept of authoritarianism as the univocal re-empowerment of a conservative, supremacist nature. Are they actually one and the same subject, the one who holds the chainsaw and the subject who wants and is capable of building a wall to safeguard the border? What histories are combined in those symbols? What are the limits and possibilities that those histories set on authoritarian imaginaries?

The difference between the image of the wall and that of the chainsaw does not only speak to the variety of marketing strategies the contemporary right can appeal to when the conjuncture calls for it. These images metabolize social dispositions, fears, and anxieties that, although they find a common denominator in the precarization of life and the loss of autonomy generated by capitalism,[38] express capitalism's internally uneven character. In essence, where the wall gives consistency to a promise of re-empowerment associated with the existence of a sovereign State sufficiently powerful to reject its foreign others, the chainsaw symbolizes the desire for omnipotence of an isolated individual who, destroying the State, hopes to see ecumenically expanded to their compatriots the precarity that currently confronts them.

The wall and the chainsaw are surely images for a false, reactive re-empowerment. But if the authoritarian ideologies of the core countries are generally based on the promise of re-empowerment *of* the State in order to "protect" the national collective figured "under threat," the Mileist pseudo-utopia is made up of quite different elements. On the one hand, in this pseudo-utopia, there isn't something like "nations" or "national" conflicts, but rather a single world, afflicted "until now" by different levels of repression/inhibition of capitalism ("social democrats," "communists," "collectivists," "Keynesians," according to the categories in use by Milei in the aforementioned Davos speech of 2024). On the other hand, there is also no "we" whom one can pretend to protect; instead, the promise of agency – its re-empowerment bait – is associated exclusively with lonely symbols (the lion, the person holding the chainsaw, the economic expert, the financial trader). Furthermore, in "chainsaw capitalism" the situation of crisis does not emerge as something to be overcome by a new state of harmony, but rather appears as consubstantial with the nature of humankind and capitalism itself, and, as such, as something to be desired and as the fulfillment of a promise.[39]

When Milei claims that in a truly unrepressed capitalism finally free from shackles we will *all* be free to sell our organs in the market[40] – that is to say, to bring the chainsaw to our own bodies – Milei [*mi-ley*][41] gives up on the classic legitimation strategy of capitalism where the crisis appears as a "moment," as an exceptional, fleeting state that we are trying to minimize. He also does not subscribe to the division of the world into geographic regions or to the formulation of alliances established by territorial criteria. If it is true that we are not dealing with an optimistic fantasy of unlimited circulation as we were in the 1990s, the idea of unrepressed capitalism that Milei upholds shares with that earlier fantasy – as it does with meritocratic individualist ideology – the most absolute indifference with respect to the existing divisions within "global capitalism." Neither his policies nor the fantasies propelled by his rhetoric point to the building of walls, to establishing limits – whether spatial, temporal, or moral. His seduction is linked, by contrast, to a normalizing of crisis, to a certain oceanic feeling of borderlessness.

The chainsaw is borderless. If the wall promises to safeguard the people it does not destroy, the chainsaw announces – on the contrary – that eventually it will destroy us all and encourages the celebration of destruction as synonymous with freedom. The solution that it proposes to the experience of powerlessness is not only immediate and reactive, to the extent that it subjectivizes the causes of the ills and aggravates the affects of resentment while preventing any action that would ameliorate the actual structural causes, as Lowenthal and Guterman argued. It is also radically incapable of imagining as real any other experience that is not that of the isolated, deterritorialized individual in a perpetual state of struggling to survive. So, whereas the subject envisioned by the supremacist at the other end of the wall is a foreigner whose expulsion is supposed to guarantee the reconquest of peace within, on the other side of the "parasites" whom the chainsaw seeks to vanquish – parasites who could include anyone deemed as such by the leader – there is no positive figuration of a situated collective, nor any promise of social reconciliation to be achieved after the vanquishing. And the fact is that the success of "unrepressed capitalism" would seem to be based less on its capacity to provide "imaginative compensations" for the cruelty of the world than in its capacity to enable emotional discharges for an anxiety that the leader makes it their business to constantly renew. The active capacity to produce shelterlessness is the sole truth of freedom. The destruction of protections is the end, not the means. And the declaration of crude interest in self-preservation is not something to be ashamed of or that needs to be dressed in the language of "national interest" or "human interest." Milei's discourse does not feature those warm expressions of "human interest" that according to Lowenthal and Guterman provide "emotional compensation for those whose life is cold and dreary, especially for those who must live a routinized and atomized existence."[42] Unrepressed capitalism is devoid of all compensatory, humanist "warmth." And this distances it not only from certain familial strategies of the neoliberal, conservative Right at the global level, but also from the cult of austere yet healthily harmonious domesticity that was upheld, before the pandemic, by Milei's current ally Mauricio Macri.

Like those illegal detention camps where "the disappeared" were sent by the Latin American dictatorships of the 1970s, Milei's chainsaw constitutes a particularly extreme image of capitalist authoritarianism configured, in this case, as unlimited, planned shelterlessness, which obtains its force not from a will to preservation but, on the contrary, from the terror or the fascination that may arise from the certainty that nothing will be safe from the destruction brought about by an all-powerful machine. Neither Chile nor Argentina, however, is a mere peripheral anomaly of capitalism. In the same way that Pinochet's ferocity gave cover to the familiarity of his neoliberal policies, Milei's eccentricity and his messianic ways are misleading insofar as they distract us from the profound market conservatism of a permanent agitation that leaves the dominant mode of production intact at a global level and deepens the concentration of capital in the hands of a few in accord with international trends. That said, the very fact that there are geographies that actually work as fields of experimentation while others do not constitutes an index of the false homogeneity of a "universal" tendency. It also marks the internally uneven character of the "globe," an image that in Latin America is associated less with a new avatar of the cosmopolitan dream than with the nightmarish specter of colonialism.

There is No Neutrality in the "Globe": A Brief History as Seen from the Southern Cone

Adorno used to say that language is hostile to what is singular, and yet it is aimed at its salvation.[43] Just as Benjamin spoke of the necessity of learning to be astonished by the terms that are for "us" the most familiar,[44] Adorno was thinking about the uneasy relation that a genuinely critical theory must entertain with the very language in which it is formulated. This is an old topos of German Romanticism, as well as of the Argentine essay tradition, from Ezequiel Martínez Estrada to Horacio González. If we had to translate it into a formula, we could say that the "metacritical" disposition demands a "linguistic imagination" capable of daring to create new terms and redeem others that have long been forgotten. At the basis of that capacity lies a suspicion: our most consolidated metaphors tend to reproduce a series of asymmetries and to impose a series of almost imperceptible blockages to the creation of a transformed world, even when they are driven by a transformative intention.

I take this to be the case with the metaphors of the "global" in expressions such as "global South," "global North," or "global authoritarianism." Despite the explicit critical intentions with which these expressions are invoked, their efficacy seems to depend on the systematic forgetting of what the "globe" means and meant for countries in the "periphery." And, thus, these propositions unconsciously make room for the kind of geopolitical imaginaries that would seem to prosper in a discourse such as Milei's. Thus, the critique of chainsaw capitalism has a radical sense that is somewhat distant from the Eurocentrism that pervades the debate between the friends and foes of Brussels.

Seen from the Southern Cone of America, there is no "globe" independently of the political definition of the continent's nations as providers of raw material in the world market and as chronic debtors of international credit entities – a definition that recalls, in turn, the international division of labor set during colonial times. Taking as the point of departure the history of post-dictatorial Argentina, we might say that there is no "globe" here without the re-primarization of the economy, the indiscriminate opening to imports, and the acquisition of foreign debt that the democratically elected government of Carlos Menem promoted during the 1990s, in continuity with the neoliberal economic policies advanced by the last civil–military dictatorship between 1976 and 1983. But we must go even further back since not only was the search for the country's "global insertion" in subordinate terms immune to the changes in political forms from dictatorship to democracy, but also its genealogy can be traced back to the process of colonization of the continent during the 16th and 17th centuries and during the liberal foundation of the nation-state toward the end of the 19th century under the slogan "Argentina, the granary of the world." Essentially, in light of this critical genealogy of the Argentine nation-state's insertion in the world economic system, there is no "globe" without colonialism; without the genocide of indigenous peoples during the "Conquest of the Desert" promoted by the liberal "generation of 1880"; without military dictatorships during the 20th century; and without the privatizing neoliberalism that around the turn of the last century and then during Mauricio Macri's government handed over the national public companies to international financial capital and sought to isolate matters of political economy from the public democratic debate in order to turn them into technical or exclusively business questions.

Therefore, from this situated critical perspective, the "globe" is not the name for an internationalist utopia, nor the name for an external threat that might come to corrupt a harmonious interior – as the anti-globalist right-wing movements in Europe claim – but above all the symbol of a suppressed internal conflict. To put it in Adornian terms, the "globe" is the figure of a "falsely reconciled totality" that is constituted by erasing the asymmetries which exist between nations, as well as within them, not to mention the existence of struggles, movements, and projects that, in Latin American nations, sought and continue to seek to challenge that controlled, politically administered inequality which is coterminous with (neo)liberal, (neo)colonial capitalism. All this erasing of conflict and inequality is the necessary condition for the "globe," a falsely harmonious image whose composition in Argentina required, nonetheless, a set of demonizations produced under the sign of political liberalism.

In effect, as we saw in chapter 6, along with the defense of the "ideology of the globe," Argentine right-wing movements elaborated a systematic denunciation of the national culture and of the "isolationism" that, as far as they were concerned, characterizes all of the popular governments, derogatorily called "populist" due to the centrality that they awarded to the internal market and due to the confrontation that they often orchestrated with those social sectors that benefited from the exportation of raw material and from financial markets. Following a historical tendency established by the local liberalism, Mauricio Macri's government denigrated the national culture as idle and conflictive, and questioned "the populisms that isolate us from the world," placing obstacles to the export of commodities and undermining Argentina's "healthy" relationship with the global market for political reasons. But he also framed those arguments in a denialist vein by associating the so-called isolationism with an alleged national obsession with death and the past. This, Macri claimed, was one of the "Argentine cultural sicknesses" – an obsession which becomes evident, according to him, in the struggle undertaken by human rights movements to bring to trial and punish those responsible for state terrorism.[45]

If we elide this long history of affinities – between "the defense of life," the forgetting of genocides, and the re-vindication of the globe; between "overcoming isolationism" and the undermining of human rights movements; between *openness* to the "world" and the celebration of the *closing* of the present upon itself – the critique of Mileism will be limited to the critique of a leader's eccentricities, provided that the Argentine case is not simply subsumed under a "general concept" of authoritarianism developed to interpret its European and American counterparts, in which case the persistence of imperialism will be rendered invisible yet again. In any case, this would not allow us to understand the phenomenon in its "peripheric" specificity. If, today, elected officials of the parliamentary alliance that stands for an "unrepressed capitalism" in Argentina can visit the imprisoned genocidaires of the last dictatorship to request their freedom, it is on the basis of this old ideological web in which the call for openness to the "globe" was never a limit for state terror denialism, but rather one of its better alibis, readily invoked without having to relinquish its democratic appearances. Therein lies one of the reasons why in Argentina the struggles in defense of human rights, workers' rights, or civil, political rights generally avoided the appeal to the figure of the "global." Translating those situated political experiences into a more theoretical language, we could say that, from a non-Eurocentric critical perspective, it would not be possible to speak of the "global" in "global authoritarianism" without addressing the fact that the term "global" is, too, an ideology whose basic operation consists in unknowing the fractured, unequal character of the "globe" – an ideology that in the region, moreover, is upheld precisely by authoritarian, denialist, neocolonial, and extractivist movements.

The debate over authoritarianism in the singular or authoritarianisms in the plural cannot be separated from the debate over the relation between authoritarianism(s) and capitalism(s). Given that it is in the name of a "full capitalism" – and not in terms of continuity with or reformulation of "neoliberalism" – that this authoritarianism acts today in Argentina, it is more important than ever to not dissociate those two terms, for both theoretical and political reasons. The fractured character of the globe – which the ideology of globalization elides – does not express just any division, but, rather, fundamentally the division installed with the capitalist international division of labor, which assigns to different regions, races, and cultures different functions in the "globe." It is due to the production and exploitation of this fracture that a global capitalism works. Just as the commodity works "not despite" but "because" of its dual character, global capitalism works "not despite" but "because" it is divided and, simultaneously, manages to erase this division, framing it as an unworked division. Faced with this mechanism, it might be possible to imagine that – in addition to refusing both to validate the "universality" of authoritarianism and to consider the emergence of authoritarianisms as a set of isolated cases – a key task of critical theory today would be to rethink that diversity as the effect of *the same* dominant geopolitical relation established *by* capitalism and on which its reproduction continues to depend.

Notes

Foreword

1 Michel Foucault, *Discipline and Punish: The Birth of the Prison*, trans. Alan Sheridan, Vintage, 1977.
2 Rosa Luxemburg, *The Russian Revolution*, trans. Bertram Wolfe, Workers Age Publishers, 1940, Chapter 6, at: https://www.marxists.org/archive/luxemburg/1918/russian-revolution/ch06.htm.

Introduction: How Are We to Read Contemporary Neoliberalism?

1 Theodor W. Adorno, "Introduction to Benjamin's *Schriften*," in *Notes to Literature*, ed. Rolf Tiedemann, trans. Shierry Weber Nicholsen, Columbia University Press, 2019, p. 479.
2 Louis Althusser, "Ideology and Ideological State Apparatus," in *Lenin and Philosophy and Other Essays*, trans. Ben Brewster, Monthly Review Press, 2001, p. 92.
3 Frankfurt Institute for Social Research, *Aspects of Sociology*, trans. John Viertel, Beacon, 1972, p. 198.
4 As María Pía López once said, in a strictly political sense, at a book presentation I attended, alluding critically to certain partisan formations that were blocking the militant sensibility to listen to the dense plot of Argentine politics.
5 Walter Benjamin, "Theses on the Philosophy of History," in

Illuminations, ed. Hannah Arendt, trans. Harry Zohn, Schocken Books, 2007, pp. 253–63.

6 Partial versions of these ideas can be found in different journals dedicated to cultural critique and political analysis: chapter 1 returns to reflections published in *Intersecciones* (January 2018); chapter 3 reformulates ideas published in *Argumentos* (No. 21, 2019); chapter 7 reworks a polemic published in *Atenea* by the Universidad de Concepción in Chile (No. 522, December 2020); and, finally, an earlier version of chapter 8 appeared in *El ojo mocho (otra vez)* in December 2019.

7 Ezequiel Martínez Estrada, *¿Qué es esto? Catilinaria*, Biblioteca Nacional, 2005.

Chapter 1 Neoliberalism's Inflections and the Triumph of the Punitive Imagination

1 Fredric Jameson, *The Cultural Turn: Selected Writings on the Postmodern, 1983–1998*, Verso, 2009.

2 Slavoj Žižek, "Multiculturalism, Or, the Cultural Logic of Multinational Capitalism," *New Left Review*, I/225, Sept./Oct. 1997, p. 36.

3 Wendy Brown, "Neoliberalism and the End of Liberal Democracy," in *Edgework: Critical Essays on Knowledge and Politics*, Princeton University Press, 2005, pp. 37–59.

4 In 2017, after being in office for two years, President Macri defeated the main opposition party in legislative elections, winning in constituencies that historically favored Peronism. This validation of a right-wing party in the country, as well as the party's much-touted pro-dialogue rhetoric, was interpreted as a sign that there was a radical discontinuity with previous right-wing administrations. In Argentina, up to this point, the Right had been strongly linked to coups d'état and support for various military dictatorships.

5 On this issue, I can heartily recommend Andrés Tzeiman, *Radiografía política del macrismo*, Caterva, 2017, including the prologue by Martín Cortés.

6 Étienne Balibar: "We might say that symmetry, whether it is that of 'adversaries' or of bodies in the political space (society, the state), carries the mortal danger of neutralizing the political and 'active' citizenship itself. We can see this in the history of contemporary socialism, which began with an effort by the labor movement (and by the working class itself) to rise up from its 'subaltern' position, to overcome exclusion (whether this was exclusion from elementary social rights or from political representation), and arrived at a

symmetry of a struggle of 'class against class,' and more precisely of 'bourgeois states' against 'proletarian states,' which became symmetrical 'camps' at the international level. A fair amount of interest given to Machiavelli by contemporary theoreticians of 'radical democracy' relates to the conceptual and symbolic tools that he provides for imagining 'democratic transformation' in which symmetry would be indefinitely deferred" (Étienne Balibar, *Citizenship*, trans. Thomas Scott-Railton, Polity, 2015, pp. 100–1).

7 Appealing to this term, Diego Tatián writes: "We propose to understand democratization as an increase in the rights of popular sectors, which had been disenfranchised of them by the relations of domination that they are typically subject to: the conquest of *civil and political rights*, whose democratic development prospers in an always provisional conquest of *social rights*, which are at the same time extended into economic rights that complement or actualize civil liberties – without which there's no democracy – with social justice and real equality – without which there's also no actual democracy, only democracy as mask and management of privilege. What is currently happening in Argentina, as in other countries in the region (Brazil) where those who are disenfranchised are further excluded and divested of rights, is what I would call a process of 'de-democratization' – and not dictatorship" ("Des-Democracia," *Relámpagos/Agencia Paco Urondo*, December 9, 2017.)

8 *Translator's note:* Kirchnerism refers broadly to the political project of the administrations of Néstor Kirchner (2003–7) and Cristina Fernández de Kirchner (2007–15).

9 One can highlight a number of acts of repression deployed by Macri's government, as documented in the March 1, 2018 report of the Centro de Estudios Legales y Sociales (CELS, Center for Legal and Social Studies). There were recurrent episodes targeting the indigenous group Wichi in Chaco and Formosa provinces, sugar mill workers in Salta and Jujuy provinces, and various Mapuche communities in Chubut, Río Negro, and Neuquén provinces, in the context of which human rights activists Santiago Maldonado (missing for 78 days) and Rafael Nahuel (shot in the back) died. There was the violent eviction of teachers who, as a form of protest for wage increases, set up a provisional school in front of the National Congress in Buenos Aires during the first months of 2017. There was also the repression and/or apprehension of protestors participating in the International Women's Strike of 2017; in the protests of social movements in front of the Ministerio de Desarrollo Social de la Nación (National Ministry of Social Development) of that same year; and in the mobilizations demanding the safe return of Santiago Maldonado, as well as the mobilizations against the Ley de Reforma

Provisional that took place in the city of Buenos Aires in December 2017. In those days, one could observe a spectacular show of military force, which included parades of police officers and gendarmerie, water cannons, and the indiscriminate "hunting" of protestors. [*Translator's note:* the mobilizations demanding the safe return of Santiago Maldonado echoed the signature demand of the Mothers of Plaza de Mayo ("*aparición con vida*," "we want them back alive"), whose children were disappeared by the military dictatorship.]

10 Mark Fisher, *Capitalist Realism: Is There No Alternative?*, Zero Books, 2009.

11 William Davies, "The New Neoliberalism," *New Left Review*, 101, Sept./Oct. 2016, pp. 121–34.

12 Walter Benjamin, "Paralipomena to 'On the Concept of History,'" in *Selected Writings, Volume 4: 1938–1940*, ed. Michael W. Jennings, trans. Edmund Jephcott and Howard Eiland, Harvard University Press, 2003, p. 406.

13 In the case of Europe, which Davies focuses on, it is a matter of "economic irrationalities" linked to credit-spurred growth and the subsequent issuing of debt whose "irrationality" demands, as necessary punishment, a painful expiation. In Argentina, however, during the period 2003–15, we witnessed a substantive cycle of foreign debt payment. This implies a significant difference with respect to the case studies that Davies analyzes to theorize punitive neoliberalism. Rather than in the extravagance of a prior indebtedness, the guilt structure set up by a punitive neoliberalism in Argentina must be thought, on the one hand, as a function of the imperative of unlimited capitalization – before which every subjective effort to take advantage of "opportunities" must fail – and, in a more political register, as a function of the break with "normality" associated with inclusive policies and the effort to strengthen the domestic market, which characterized progressive governments in the region during the first decade and a half of this century. As we will see in chapter 5, this break with what was thought of as "the natural order of things" was experienced by certain segments of the population as unbearable anarchy.

14 See note 9 above.

15 See, in particular, Althusser's comments in *On the Reproduction of Capitalism: Ideology and Ideological State Apparatuses*, trans. G.M. Goshgarian, Verso, 2014.

16 Carrió's rhetoric of guilt expiation and punishment has remained constant throughout her career. She combines demands for legal justice with calls for the moral and spiritual purification of Argentine society in order to finally put an end to the ethical decadence that, according to her, has been pervasive for decades. See, for instance,

her reference to the "divine lesson" to be imparted on Kirchnerism over an alleged electoral fraud in 2015: "Carrió denuncia que 'están construyendo el fraude,'" *eldoce.tv*, August 9, 2015. And, more recently, her appeal to atone for the moral corruption of the nation: "El mensaje 'místico' de Elisa Carrió a los argentinos," *Perfil*, July 14, 2022.

17 See María Eugenia Vidal, *Mi camino*, Sudamericana, 2021. A critical commentary by Daniel Rosso, "Vidal: La lucha contra el demonio," can be found at *lateclaenerevista.com*, June 2, 2021. For an interesting study of the iconography of Vidal's political campaigns, see Germán Rosso: "Inocencia, pureza y abnegación. La construcción de la imagen de María Eugenia Vidal en las elecciones de la provincia de Buenos Aires, Argentina (2015)," *Revista Sociedad*, No. 45, Facultad de Ciencias Sociales, Universidad de Buenos Aires, pp. 153–79.

18 See "Para Michetti hay un 'despilfarro de 34 años,'" *Página 12*, November 30, 2017.

19 In *The Authoritarian Personality* (see T.W. Adorno, Else Frenkel-Brunswik, Daniel J. Levinson, and R. Nevitt Sanford, *The Authoritarian Personality*, Science Editions, 1964), Adorno defines authoritarian submission as a "submissive, uncritical attitude toward idealized moral authorities of the ingroup" and authoritarian aggression as the "tendency to be on the lookout for, and to condemn, reject and punish people who violate conventional values" (p. 248). Both authoritarian submission and authoritarian aggression constitute variables of "The F Scale," formulated to tally the often unconscious authoritarian tendencies in a population.

20 See chapter 5 of this book.

21 Milagro Sala, activist and leader of the organization Túpac Amaru, was detained for participating in a protest outside of the government seat in Jujuy on January 16, 2016, right before Mauricio Macri began his term. She remains in prison. Her arrest was widely touted in the media as proof of the corruption and violence of social movements. In 2016, a United Nations Working Group called her arrest arbitrary. In 2017, the Inter-American Court of Human Rights ordered that Argentina immediately adopt the necessary measures to protect Sala's life and health. According to Amnesty International, "After her arrest, a flurry of 'consecutive accusations', the deployment of legal cases and weakened judicial independence all combined to uphold the decision to keep Sala imprisoned indefinitely" (see https://amnistia.org.ar/noticias/milagro-sala-cuatro-anos-de-detencion-arbitraria).

22 Amado Boudou, vice-president of Argentina during Cristina Fernández de Kirchner's second term (2011–15), was detained

in November 2017 and charged with embezzlement. Boudou's arrest took place late at night and images of him barefoot and in pajamas circulated widely in the media (see https://www.youtube.com/watch?v=TBemZkxFVds). After Boudou's spectacular arrest, several organizations and political leaders expressed concern over a tendency of Argentinian judicial power to use preventive detention against politicians of the previous administration, exposing them in the process to a media circus. After Boudou's conviction, these organizations and leaders characterized his trial and imprisonment as an example of lawfare. See "Libertad a Amado Boudou," *Página 12*, January 11, 2021.

Chapter 2 Cruel Freedom

1 Theodor W. Adorno, *Aesthetic Theory*, trans. Robert Hullot-Kentor, Continuum, 1970, p. 245.
2 Theodor W. Adorno, *Problems of Moral Philosophy*, ed. Thomas Schröder, trans. Rodney Livingstone, Stanford University Press, 2001.
3 In proposing the term "de-autonomy," I am echoing Diego Tatián's argument about "de-democratization," cited in the previous chapter.
4 See Judith Butler, *Notes Toward a Performative Theory of Assembly*, Harvard University Press, 2018.
5 In *Undoing the Demos: Neoliberalism's Stealth Revolution* (Zone Books, 2015), Wendy Brown demonstrates that the market logic, expanded by neoliberalism through every domain of life, destroys a certain internal plurality in the modern individual, eroding the possibility of the emergence of the autonomous subject. While in classic liberalism, *Homo economicus* described the rationality imputed to the individual as economic agent, in neoliberalism this becomes extended as a mode of subjectivation that knows no limits or conflicts with moral principles stemming from other spheres of one's life. We will come back to this argument, as well as to its possible limits, in the next chapter.
6 Max Horkheimer, *Critical Theory: Selected Essays*, trans. Matthew J. O'Connell et al., Continuum, 2002, p. 232. [*Translator's note:* In the translation from which Catanzaro quotes, "opposition" is "*resistencia*" and "independence" is "*autonomía.*"]
7 Theodor W. Adorno and Max Horkheimer, *Towards a New Manifesto*, trans. Rodney Livingstone, Verso, 2019, pp. 4–5.
8 See "Alejandro Rozitchner: 'El pensamiento crítico es un valor negativo,'" *La Nación*, December 20, 2016. As far as the anti-intellectual stances of the head of the government are concerned, here is

a lengthy fragment from one of his first interviews upon assuming office: "I think the 21st century arranged ideologies in terms of results. People want to live better, they want to have a healthy life, they want to be hyperconnected, they want to project a future for their kids, so they are searching for someone who can promise those things. Then there is a minority who want to relate all of that with histories, with reasons, and philosophers. . . But the truth is that, at the end of the day, what matters is my son. Will he have a better future than I did? In other words, that narcissistic love one channels through one's kids. People want guarantees, so that's what they're searching for." See "He tenido días de abrumarme," *Perfil*, March 20, 2016. For an interesting reflection on this interview, see Horacio González, "Filosofía, filialidad y 'vida sana,'" *agenciapacouurondo.com*, March 22, 2016.

9 See Luciana Vázquez, "Educación: ¿vale la pena ir a la universidad?," *La Nación*, March 18, 2016.

10 Referring to the central role played by family relations in the rhetoric of Macri's political party, González remarked on the alienation of symbols and historical debates brought about by the flattening of language to the sphere of domesticity, which the government held to be more authentic, spontaneous, and unproblematic. See González, "Filosofía, filialidad y 'vida sana.'"

11 Fredric Jameson, *The Cultural Turn: Selected Writings on the Postmodern, 1983–1998*, Verso, 2009.

12 See, among others, Mark Fisher, *Capitalist Realism: Is There No Alternative?*, Zero Books, 2009; Colin Crouch, *Post-Democracy*, Polity, 2004; Wolfgang Streeck, *How Will Capitalism End? Essays on a Failing System*, London: Verso, 2016.

13 Slavoj Žižek, *The Sublime Object of Ideology*, Verso, 2009 [1989].

14 María Pía López, "Los años despiadados. Notas sobre el pasado reciente," *El ojo mocho*, 16, 2001, p. 90.

15 Lauren Berlant, *Cruel Optimism*, Duke University Press, 2011, p. 24, emphases in original.

16 The neocolonial resonances of this discourse are explored in chapter 6, where I propose the necessity of modulating, in the context of a necessary critique of nationalist and xenophobic discourses, the political potential of "the nation," whether invoked to advance supremacist geopolitical positions or to articulate historically subordinated positions.

17 I take my distance from those critiques that emphasize the excessive optimism of Macri's government and highlight as one of its essential features the hyperinflation of its promissory dimension. The constant pronouncements about an imminent improvement of the economy, which never happened but that nonetheless was

a recurrent feature of the presidency up until the end, should be understood not as promises relative to a future to come, but rather as discursive rituals that did not intend to become reality and that precisely because of that were not refutable when they did not come to pass. As systems of confirmation, rather than anticipating an effectively different future-present, these rituals sought to confirm that the only thing that truly exists is what already is.

18 Wendy Brown, "Neoliberalism's Frankenstein: Authoritarian Freedom in Twenty-First Century 'Democracies,'" *Critical Times*, Vol. 1, No. 1, January 2018, pp. 60–79.

19 In his reflection on conventionalism as it relates to the authoritarian personality, Adorno shows that rigidity and flexibility are far from being polar opposites. According to him, the kind of subject in question "could in good conscience follow the dictates of the external agency wherever they might lead him and, moreover, he would be capable of totally exchanging one set of standards for another quite different one" (T.W. Adorno, Else Frenkel-Brunswik, Daniel J. Levinson, and R. Nevitt Sanford, *The Authoritarian Personality*, Science Editions, 1964, p. 230). It is this fluctuation, or interchangeability, of values that actually constitutes for Adorno the correlative to rigidity and not its antidote, despite what a pro-dialogue ideology might imagine. If, in the latter, flexibility assumes a supposedly anti-totalitarian and democratic value of adaptation without limits, this absence of limits, this indifference, constitutes for Adorno, in fact, a sign of rigidity in a potentially authoritarian consciousness that, in its very malleability, reveals its petrification. In this sense, "conventional" means not only holding on to a determinate position that could come into conflict with others, but also that indifference and adaptability in relation to all the positions harmoniously upheld by the average common sense. In other words, "conventionalist" would be that over-adapted consciousness which lacks autonomy and adheres rigidly to whatever position, regardless of its substance.

Chapter 3 Is the Critique of Ideology Obsolete?

1 Frankfurt Institute for Social Research, *Aspects of Sociology*, trans. John Viertel, Beacon, 1972, p. 189. By emphasizing the fact that an ideology is both *suffered* and *of use*, the concept of ideology – even as false consciousness (in, for example, Georg Lukács, *History and Class Consciousness: Studies in Marxist Dialectics*, trans. Rodney Livingstone, MIT Press, 1971) – warns against the reductive interpretation of justifications as merely instrumentalist

and rationalistic. As a component of "false consciousness," justification does not lead back to a sovereign subject without at the same time placing that subject in the web of passivity proper to action as such. So, for instance, if in the political philosophers of the social contract tradition a certain evolutionary thinking (or *telos*) *works* as justification for the slavery that a nascent capitalism cannot avoid and must actually encourage, that evolutionary thinking represents simultaneously a *limit of that philosophical consciousness*, incapable of transcending a linear representation of time that imagines capitalism as the overcoming of slavery.

2 Frankfurt Institute for Social Research, *Aspects of Sociology*, pp. 190–1.

3 I take my distance from Žižek when he subscribes to the idea that Adorno reduces ideology to its doctrinarian dimension and interprets National Socialism as an operation beyond ideology, as sheer acts of coercion, instead of reading its actions as effective rituals in which a crucial dimension of ideology, usually ignored by rationalistic approaches, was actualized (see Slavoj Žižek, "The Spectre of Ideology," in *Mapping Ideology*, Verso, 2012, p. 13). As we will see, Adorno argues that the truly doctrinal dimension of ideology is modern and liberal: it presupposes an enlightened confidence and, at the same time, attests to the fact that this has already come into crisis, and, for that reason, this confidence must be thematized, needing argumentation to sustain itself. But this does not mean that in the Adornian conception this doctrinal dimension is ideology *tout court*, or that, as the "bourgeois spirit" wanes, another ideological dimension could not occupy center stage. In fact, in the passage quoted, in referring to "human dispositions" over which discourses operate through a work with form and beyond all manifest content, Adorno is suggesting precisely that historical shift in the prominent forms of ideology.

4 *Translator's note*: in some English editions of *Capital* (Volume 1), for example the 1976 Ben Fowkes translation from Penguin, the primitive accumulation chapter is XXVI. In other editions, such as the 2024 Princeton University Press edition (translated by Paul Reitter), and in the Spanish translation with which Catanzaro works, it is chapter XXIV.

5 Marx: "Along with the constant decrease in the number of capitalist magnates, who usurp and monopolize all the advantages of this process of transformation, the mass of misery, oppression, slavery, degradation and exploitation grows; but with this there also grows the revolt of the working class, a class constantly increasing in numbers, and trained, united and organized by the very mechanism of the capitalist process of production" (Karl Marx, *Capital Volume*

1, trans. Ben Fowkes, Penguin, 1976, p. 929). [*Translator's note*: in the Penguin edition of *Capital*, which works with the fourth edition of *Capital* supervised by Engels, this quote is found in chapter 32.]

6 We know, Althusser says, that the feudal class recognized itself in Christian religious ideology, much like the bourgeois class in the period of its classic domination recognized itself in legal ideology. "The working class, for its part, recognizes itself [. . .] above all in an *ideology of a political kind:* not in bourgeois political ideology (class domination), but in proletarian political ideology, that of class struggle for the abolition of classes and the construction of communism" (*On the Reproduction of Capitalism,* pp. 228–9, original emphasis). Despite the accusations of scientistic reductionism aimed also at Althusser, among readers of Marx it was he who emphasized the irreducible and meaningfully fraught multiplicity of the term "class struggle" in the Marxist tradition: first, in the sense of it being something "eternal," insofar as everything existing was already an effect of class struggle; second, in the sense of a possibility of resistance and transformation for which one must agitate because it might not come to be; and, finally, the sense of constituting an *ideology in which the working class recognizes itself*. In effect, quite unlike the emphases on dis-identification or the deconstruction of collective identities, as well as the unilateral, unequivocal affirmation of dispossession, destitution, and impropriety that one finds in critics such as Robert Esposito and Giorgio Agamben – and that permeate relevant contributions to contemporary political-philosophical thought in France and elsewhere (see, for example, Vladimir Safatle, *O circuito dos Afectos: Corpos políticos, desamparo e o fim do indivíduo*, Cosac Naify, 2015) – Althusser always understood the pretension to situate oneself beyond identity and ideology as itself ideological and rejected its viability as a model of emancipatory practice. His position turns out to be truer in a moment when precisely the dominant ideology – unlike during May 1968 in France, no longer an adequate horizon for our period – demands flexibility of all identity and treats fluidity as coterminous with a healthy relation to the unappealable demands of the system. As Eduardo Grüner points out: "The thought ranged under the banner *post* has understandably reacted against the monstrosities committed in the 20th century in the name of various sorts of identitarian substantialisms – genocides, 'ethnic cleansings,' mass annihilations – by favoring 'connections,' 'hybridity,' those *in-between* (as [Homi K.] Bhabha would say), etc. But this valorization of *connectivity* has been accompanied with an enormous distrust – or open rejection – toward the very idea of *collectivity*, or, worse, *community*, ideas which became in themselves suspected of

essentialism (whether national, class, or religious). Any 'solid' social formation is labeled as potentially 'totalitarian' and sent to the hell of a socially nefarious, dangerous thought" (Eduardo Grüner, *Lo sólido en el aire: el eterno retorno de la crítica marxista*, CLACSO, 2021, p. 381).

7 Žižek, "The Spectre of Ideology."

8 Étienne Balibar, *Citizenship*, trans. Thomas Scott-Railton, Polity, 2015, chapter 7.

9 Following Balibar's argument in his critique of Brown, I consider that the neoliberal flattening of the conditions of possibility of subjective autonomy that Brown has so acutely described should be understood not as a consummate ethical destitution but as a tendency, in conflict with others, and capable of being thematized by appealing to the Althusserian concept of ideology. As I will argue in chapter 5, the neoliberalization of life would be appreciable, in that sense, less as a full capture of the subject in subjection than as the dominance, in a determinate conjuncture, of a certain social sensibility, more diffuse and incoherent than a doctrine, that operates mainly as lived experience, constituting and manifesting itself through practices, dispositions, presuppositions, and subjective passions that are not necessarily coherent or conscious. It is an ideological sensibility or sensible ideology that, in turn, responds to – and coexists with – elements that contradict it and sustain with it a conflict of variable intensity.

10 I refer to the limits associated with a type of questioning that takes ideology as a pure deficit of knowledge, a deficit that could and should be overcome. As we saw earlier, Marx accounts for these limits when he refers to the emergence of a practice that would necessarily involve, even in a world transformed, an ideological dimension: the political practice of an emancipatory nature.

11 Would it not be possible to see something like the Marxian avowal of tension – between humanist critique of representations and analysis of performative effects – in the Derridean postulation of justice as the limit of a deconstruction that is irreducible to pure analytical immanence; or in the Althusserian persistence, despite his anti-humanist stand, in the semantic field of the critique of exploitation; or in that which Adorno meant by the idea of a *life*, not bare but *damaged*, and what Benjamin had in mind with the image of a weak *messianic* force insisting upon history?

12 I do not agree with Žižek when he distinguishes so neatly between ritual and belief, associating the former with ideology decreed "from above" by the State – whose paradigmatic example would be the Ideological State Apparatuses conceptualized by Althusser – and the latter with a spontaneous ideology stemming "from below," as

subjects participate in the Market, exemplified by the Lukácsian reinterpretation of commodity fetishism. While it may help us to distinguish between the preferred objects of analysis, political or sociological, respectively (for instance, the difference between a political science interested in mutations in discourse and political institutions, and a sociological interest in the forms of labor organization and its effects on subjectivity), this distinction tends to obfuscate what they both have in common as machine-like and external mechanisms, productive of subjective effects, and structurally opaque for an individual conscience that seeks to represent them as they work. See Žižek's argument in "The Spectre of Ideology."

13 See, on the articulation of ideology and the unconscious in Louis Althusser, "Three Notes on the Theory of Discourse," in *The Humanist Controversy and Other Writings*, ed. François Matheron, trans. G.M. Goshgarian, Verso, 2003, pp. 33–84. Let's remember that for Althusser this relation has a double aspect. On the one hand, the subjective recognition of an ideological interpellation involves an unknowing, an unconscious element on the part of the subject, with respect to the performative character of an appeal that creates subjects by presupposing them ("Only a 'subject presumed to exist' is ever interpellated," ibid., p. 55). On the other hand, the unconscious is articulated with, exists in, ideological formations, and does so in a selective manner: "the unconscious (a given unconscious) does not function on just any formation of the ideological, but only on certain formations, those so configured that the mechanisms of the unconscious can 'come into play' in them, and the formations of the unconscious can 'take hold' in them. To go back to a metaphor used above: a given engine does not run on just anything, but on petrol if it is a petrol engine, and so on" (ibid., p. 59).

14 In this way, the role of the argumentative capacities of subjects that a pragmatic sociology has studied (see, for instance, Luc Boltanski and Laurent Thévenot, *On Justification: Economies of Worth*, trans. Catherine Porter, Princeton University Press, 2006) should not be confidently absolutized – in a rationalist/progressive vein – or simply disavowed – in a possibly disabling radicalization of a hermeneutic of suspicion canonically deployed by writers such as Nietzsche and Freud.

Chapter 4 Paradoxes of Autonomy (and Its Critique): Judith Butler and Theodor Adorno

1 Theodor W. Adorno, "Messages in a Bottle," trans. Edmund Jephcott, *New Left Review*, 1/200, July/Aug. 1993, p. 5.

2 Theodor W. Adorno, "Society," trans. Fredric R. Jameson, *Salmagundi*, Fall 1969–Winter 1970, pp. 152–3.
3 Adorno: "In the period of his decay, the individual's experience of himself and what he encounters contributes once more to knowledge, which he had merely obscured as long as he continued unshaken to construe himself positively as the dominant category" (Theodor W. Adorno, *Minima Moralia: Reflections on a Damaged Life*, trans. E.F.N. Jephcott, Verso, 2005, pp. 17–18).
4 Alongside this illegibility of the production of individual nullity, the falsely reconciled character of totality, the false "harmony" presupposed by liberal thought, became illegible, too.
5 Adorno, *Minima Moralia*, p. 150.
6 William Davies: "Neoliberalism has become incredible, but that is partly because it is a system that no longer seeks credibility in the way that hegemonies used to do, through a degree of cultural or normative consensus. Sovereign power has always had a circular logic, exercised to demonstrate that it can be exercised. Yet today, that sovereignty is found in technical and technocratic spheres: policies, punishments, cuts, calculations are simply being repeated, as that is the sole condition of their reality" ("The New Neoliberalism," *New Left Review*, 101, Sept./Oct. 2016, pp. 133–4). Although the thesis of an incredible present seems to me extremely suggestive, as we saw in the previous chapter with respect to Wendy Brown, one might think that the type of explanation Davies proposes for this situation must enter into a dialectic with aspects of reality that contradict it, particularly as it pertains to the diagnosis of a radical abandonment of the struggle for signification and cultural consensus on the part of elite power.
7 Walter Benjamin, "Theses on the Philosophy of History," in *Illuminations: Essays and Reflections*, trans. Harry Zohn, Schocken Books, 1968, p. 256.
8 Judith Butler, *Notes Toward a Performative Theory of Assembly*, Harvard University Press, 2018, p. 14. [*Translator's note:* the translation with which Catanzaro works has the word "*autonomía*" ("autonomy") instead of "self-sufficiency."]
9 Ibid., p. 16.
10 Ibid., p. 21.
11 Ibid., p. 25.
12 Excessively free and at the same time subjected, even on a psychic level. Butler: "if responsibility is first and foremost a responsibility to become economically self-sufficient under conditions that undermine all prospects of self-sufficiency, then we are confronted by a contradiction that can easily drive one mad: we are morally pushed to become precisely the kind of subjects who are structurally

foreclosed from realizing that norm" (ibid., p. 14). The responsibilization imposed on the individual as entrepreneur of the self in social conditions that make that mandate impossible produces a feeling of individualized anxiety and an overwhelming sense of moral failure: "The more one complies with the demand of 'responsibility' to become self-reliant, the more socially isolated one becomes and the more precarious one feels; and the more supporting social structures fall away for 'economic' reasons, the more isolated one feels in one's sense of heightened anxiety and 'moral failure'" (ibid., p. 15).

13 Ibid., p. 16.

Chapter 5 Neoliberal Sensibilities

1 Sara Ahmed, *The Cultural Politics of Emotion*, Edinburgh University Press, 2014, p. 202.

2 Wolfgang Streeck, *How Will Capitalism End? Essays on a Failing System*, Verso, 2016, p. 15, original emphasis.

3 The diagnosis of anomic individualism is objectionable in two ways. On the one hand, it tends to underestimate the power of neoliberalism to produce paradoxical forms of social ties and figures of community. On the other hand, it leaves unquestioned – or rather simply defers – the contrasting relation between individual autonomy and social justice that, precisely, the neoliberal ideology under criticism persists in projecting *as* an alternative of the kind "or this, or that." Situated along the same ideological coordinates as its object of critique, the theory meets obstacles almost insurmountable in conceptualizing and problematizing the specifically neoliberal inflections of justice. But, also, the emphasis on the individualist character of this ideology finds serious limits when it seeks to thematize the modes in which neoliberalism becomes authoritarian, damaging individual autonomy by undermining social conditions – economic, political, cultural, and psychic – that could benefit its development, and promotes not only openly repressive policies, but also anti-intellectual and culturally conservative impulses.

4 François Dubet, *Repensar la justicia social*, Siglo XXI, 2011, p. 114.

5 Ibid., p. 114.

6 Ibid., p. 116.

7 Quoted in Wendy Brown, "Neoliberalism's Frankenstein: Authoritarian Freedom in Twenty-First Century 'Democracies,'" *Critical Times*, Vol. 1, No. 1, January 2018, p. 60.

8 "Freedom" here is defined negatively and not, Brown emphasizes, as a power to act that would call for interventions and limits to be deployed in the first place.

9 Brown, "Neoliberalism's Frankenstein," p. 63.

10 An irony that points to the necessity of not taking at face value the self-presentation of neoliberalism as being in stark opposition to paternalism. While it opposes the application of social policies and regulations to economic practices geared toward welfare, the fact is that neoliberalism is in no way incompatible with paternalistic and/or infantilizing attitudes. On the contrary, as witness the neoliberal support for private charity or the steadfast defense of parental authority expressed in the now common refrain "Don't mess with my kids." The latter is typically used to ban sexual education from school curricula, where it is stigmatized as "gender ideology" – which, according to this argument, would be an ideological imposition on a more "authentic nature" – that seeks to erode parents' authority in their children's education. See Marina Carbajal, "La nueva cruzada," *Página 12*, September 17, 2018.

11 Brown, "Neoliberalism's Frankenstein," pp. 65, 66, 67.

12 Fragment from one of the focus groups conducted in CABA/Buenos Aires in January 2015, as part of the Multiyear Project of Investigation CONICET, "Problemas de la democracia argentina en el período de la post-convertibilidad. Transformaciones socioeconómicas y reconfiguraciones ideológicas" (2011–15) ("Problems of Argentinian democracy in the period of post-convertibility. Socioeconomic transformations and ideological reconfigurations"). This and other materials analyzed in this chapter were developed, as part of that investigation, by the Grupo de Estudios Críticos sobre Ideologías y Democracia (GECID), Instituto de Investigaciones Gino Germani, Universidad of Buenos Aires. [*Translator's note:* "*precios cuidados*" (careful pricing) was a government program launched by Cristina Fernández de Kirchner's administration in December 2013. The program's objective was to contain the rise in the cost of basic foods and to facilitate access to those food items by the poorest sectors. After the end of Fernández de Kirchner's administration, the program was significantly reduced, eventually including only a few products deemed absolutely necessary.]

13 For a more detailed treatment of this duality in Macri's administration, see María Stegmayer and Gisela Catanzaro, "Inflexiones del neoliberalismo y sus efectos sobre la subjetividad: imperativos y paradojas de una nueva discursividad pública en la Argentina reciente," *Revista Entramados y Perspectivas*, No. 8, 2018, pp. 4–31.

14 The almost physical experience of abuse of authority that was behind these denunciations reached fever pitch when Cristina Fernández de Kirchner's administration made the decision to limit the purchase of dollars by private individuals to $200 per month.

This measure, which had the objective to avoid depleting the national reserves of dollars, was baptized by the opposition party as "cuffing the dollar" ("*cepo al dólar*"). And, even though the decision only affected the most privileged strata of the population (who were alone able to invest in foreign currency), it created a sort of widespread panic, as if the government had forbidden the purchase of basic necessities.

15 I am referring to the conflict popularly known in Argentina as "*la 125*," in reference to the resolution that, in 2008 and during Cristina Fernández's government, sought to transform the agricultural tributary scheme in order to redistribute to the poorest sectors in society the extraordinary income generated by the agricultural sectors due to the international increase in commodity prices. Appealing to Sara Ahmed's terminology in her analysis of the constitution and political potential of social affects, we could say that, as with the restricting of the purchase of dollars, this measure ended up playing an unexpected but crucial role in the consolidation of fantasies of harassment prevalent in the dominant sectors of Argentine society – or, to put it differently, in the construction of the ordinary and normative as something in crisis, and the ordinary, normative subject as "hurt" and even damaged by the "invasion" of others. Emphasizing the social, produced character of affectivity, it is important to highlight that what we are referring to here as an unconscious disposition to decode redistributive policies as a threat, and certain indices of social transformation as "chaos" that must be rejected even by recourse to physical violence toward their alleged agents, should not be psychologized to the point of rendering illegible those emotions as subjective modes of investment in social norms rather than mere psychological attributes. In the terms Ahmed proposes to analyze the discourses of hate: the critical deployment of the concept of unconscious emotivity should not obscure the fact that "violence against others involves forms of power that are visceral and bodily, as well as social and structural" (Ahmed, *The Cultural Politics of Emotion*, p. 56).

16 Nancy Fraser, *Scales of Justice: Reimagining Political Space in a Globalizing World*, Columbia University Press, 2008, p. 128.

17 We initially conducted eight focus groups: six that followed the standard procedures associated with this genre of investigation (prior selection, Gesell Chamber, in Buenos Aires), and two in a non-controlled environment that allowed us to approach the same issues from different social contexts and that, in this case, involved two groups of older women who were imprisoned. The participants of the controlled group were separated by age (young people between 18 and 30, adults from 30 to 60, and a group of people

over 60) and according to their disposition toward democracy (pro-democracy and anti-democracy), determined through a brief questionnaire that used a sample from the poll "Problemas de la democracia Argentina," about which we will speak shortly. For the six groups in the controlled environment, we maintained the criteria of intra-group homogeneity (of age, of democratic disposition) with an eye to promoting dialogue, as well as inter-group heterogeneity in order to facilitate their comparative analysis.

18 For a study of these same materials specifically focusing on images of justice, see Micaela Cuesta and Lucía Wegelin, "Imaginarios de justicia social en las subjetividades argentinas contemporáneas," *Methaodos: Revista de ciencias sociales*, Vol. 5, No. 2, 2017, pp. 243–59. For an analysis of the "constellation of insecurity" that we traced from the quantitative data collected in that same investigation, see the article I wrote with Sebastián Elizalde and Gabriela Seghezzo: "La ideología de la inseguridad en la Argentina actual," *Revista Sociedade e Cultura*, Vol. 19, No. 1, Jan./June 2016, pp. 21–36.

19 This meritocratic criterion of justice that already in 2013 we found, as we will see, widespread among the population we surveyed constitutes one of the most distinctive characteristics of some of the surveys conducted with precarious groups in popular sectors, as evinced by the following fragment drawn from one of the focal groups from Ezeiza prison with a group of women prisoners:

> A: If someone is poor, it is because they want to be. It's as simple as that. If you want to go there, no one dies from hunger. Whoever dies from hunger it is because they want to die. Because if you have a kid and you don't have a job, you can get up and start selling whatever. I think that poor people want to be poor. Because they're used to things being handed to them. The thing is that you often see a lot of people who got used to babying their 20-year-old, who does nothing all day and doesn't even know how to wash a cup. But, why? Because you didn't teach him how to figure it out on his own.
>
> Coordinator: If a lawyer and a construction worker charged the same, what would you say to that?
>
> B: I don't think that's right either. Because a lawyer has, what, eight years, seven years of school. The guy really used his head, years passed. And a bum from the street is going to make the same amount of money?

20 A passage from fear to anger that Mariana Gainza and Ezequiel Ipar describe as follows: someone starts by imagining a fragile position that "makes" them face a threat which, from a rational perspective of the situation, is completely unreal. But then, through a strange inversion, the imaginary victim ends up embodying in their own subjectivity the violence that was previously attributed to

the object of the fantasy. Schematically, "fantasies are disseminated that figure the other (a determinate, external other) as all-powerful and overwhelming; the people affected are represented as victims of an imaginary power that, bearing no relation to the distribution of social power, goes through them intimately; fear enlivens them and they 'must' therefore turn to any means and defensive mechanisms that would safeguard them from the threat; as a result of this, they end up imitating the fantastical monster in the details of the defensive violence they profess" (Mariana Gainza and Ezequiel Ipar, "El laberinto de los afectos en el neoliberalismo," *Revista Teoría y Crítica de la Psicología*, Vol. 8, 2016, p. 249).

21 For a deeper analysis of the perspective of ideology critique we favored in that earlier study, see Ezequiel Ipar and Gisela Catanzaro (eds.), *La subjetividad antidemocrática: elementos para la crítica de las ideologías contemporáneas*, Instituto Gino Germani, Facultad de Ciencias Sociales, UBA, 2016.

22 We can observe this difference comparing, for example, the high levels of adherence with respect to statements 1, 3, and 4, and the significantly fewer negative responses to statement 2. This difference in adherence when faced with statements not so dissimilar in content shows that the unknowing of trans-subjective determinations on which subjective agency depends presents itself as, precisely, an unknowing rather than a positive, explicit affirmation of self-sufficiency as doctrinal principle consciously held by subjects.

23 To lose sight of the difference and the respective efficacy of these two levels of ideology – doctrine, explicitly and consciously held, and lived experience, social substratum relatively opaque for the individual and on which ultimately depends the validity and endurance of a determinate form of social organization – leads to two related risks. On the one hand, there is the "political science" risk of overestimating the social validity of what is stated at the doctrinal level on the part of political leaders. On the other hand, there is the risk, common across opinion polls, of considering as socially valid only that which the individual is capable of asserting at a conscious level: for instance, in opinions about racism, pluralism, democracy, and so on. If the political or doctrinaire *translation* depends on certain social conditions of possibility to achieve efficacy, it also generally requires, inversely, exacting a distance – no small feat – between unconscious dispositions that configure a certain social sensibility and the explicit and doctrinal enunciation of certain principles that would be untenable for many.

24 The correlation – that measures the strength and the direction of the relation between 2 variables or, in this case, between two items grouped in turn as variables – between the statements under

consideration has been extremely significant with the exception of the (negative) items 2 and 7. We note the existence of a statistically relevant joint variation in the case of the following items:
1 correlated with 3, 4, 5, 8, 9, 10, 11, and 12
3 with 1, 9, and 11
4 with 1, 5, 6, 8, 9, 10, 11
5 with 1, 4, 6, 8, 9, 10, 11
6 with 4, 5, 10, 11
8 with 1, 4, 5, 9, 10, 11, 12
9 with 1, 3, 4, 5, 10, 11, 12
10 with 1, 4, 5, 6, 8, 9, 11, 12
11 with 1, 3, 4, 5, 6, 8, 9, 10, 12
12 with 1, 8, 9, 10, 11

Chapter 6 Authoritarian Neoliberalism and the National Question

1 Ezequiel Martínez Estrada, *X-Ray of the Pampa*, trans. Alain Swietlicki, University of Texas Press, 1971.
2 As I will emphasize in the final chapter, while it is necessary to speak of a neoliberal "authoritarian turn" to refer to certain ideological drifts that have gained primacy in recent years on an international scale, this terminology is nonetheless problematic from a Latin American perspective, since the implementation of neoliberal economic policies in that region since the 1970s went hand in hand with dictatorial governments.
3 On the imbrication of liberalism and authoritarianism in the region, see Ezequiel Ipar, "Neoliberalismo y neoautoritarismo," *Política y Sociedad*, Vol. 55, No. 3, 2018, pp. 825–49. On punitive securitarianism, see Gabriela Seghezzo and Nicolás Dallorso, "Del punitivismo al cuidado (feminista): el porvenir de la ilusión securitaria," in Nahuel Sosa, Marina Cardelli, and Alejandro San Cristobal, *Emergencias: repensar el Estado, las subjetividades y la acción política*, Ciccus, 2018, pp. 173–83. According to them, this idea of securitarianism displaces a conception of security which was enmeshed with the idea of social protections that are owed as rights to citizens. More concretely: in punitive securitarianism, "the preoccupation over how to secure social protections is eclipsed by the imperative to neutralize the effects of the process by which these protections are cancelled" (ibid., p. 174).
4 Mauricio Macri's decree 683/2018 interrupted a sustained political effort to enshrine in state policy the non-intervention of the armed forces in tasks associated with matters of internal security. This

effort began in 1988 with the law of National Defense promulgated by the government of Raúl Alfonsín; it continued under the government of Carlos Menem with the law of internal security passed in 1992 and the law of national intelligence passed in 2001 during Fernando de la Rúa's presidency, which was eventually ratified in 2006 with the law of defense during the Néstor Kirchner administration. In line with decree 683/2018, another decree by Macri opened the door for intelligence agencies and armed forces to recover their self-government and thus shield themselves from control by democratically elected officials. As Seghezzo and Dallorso point out ("Del punitivismo al cuidado (feminista)"), through decree 217/2016, the long process of bringing the armed forces under the purview of executive power was abruptly reversed.

5 "The selectiveness produced by these forms of administration are in tension with any program that has as its objective the recognition of the right to migrate and to legalization. It involves a regressive process, where even the false classification proposed by the national Executive Power regulates in a differentiated way migrations according to the conduct of migrants." To access the report and other materials associated with migrations produced by the CELS, see https://www.cels.org.ar/web/tag/dnu-migrantes/.

6 A case that became emblematic of Macri's government's support for the actions of police, even when these operated outside the regulative frames, was what became known by locals as the "Chocobar doctrine." Toward the end of 2017, after a police agent called Luis Chocobar killed a man who had committed a robbery by shooting him in the back, the president and the minister of security received him in the house of government, endorsing his conduct. A similar gesture of unconditional support toward the armed forces took place on the occasion of the murders of Santiago Maldonado and Rafael Nahuel when they participated in protests organized by the Mapuche community in the south of the country.

7 "Defined vaguely in relation to crime and the protection of certain goods and social groups in the public space, as an urgent problem that requires urgent solutions, insecurity becomes ever more central during the 1990s. Despite the troublesome nature of this definition, as we said, the construction of the problem is based, practically without exceptions, on the strict connection between crime and popular sectors, a link that configures determinate ways of seeing, thinking, and acting, which reify a supposed connection between delinquency and poverty, and produces inequality, fragmentation, and hyper-vulnerability of the most impoverished sectors. Securitization works, and there lies its specificity, as a sort of negative pulley whose spring or axle is the activation of fear.

The '*pibe chorro*' [roughly, 'young thug'] becomes the sinister counterpart of the entrepreneur: he combines success, creativity, wit, and risk. That is, the 'pibe chorro' is an *other* but with similar values" (Nicolás Dallorso and Gabriela Seghezzo, "Apuntes para una crítica del securitarismo neoliberal en Argentina" (2021), available at: https://ri.conicet.gov.ar/handle/11336/200018.

8 "I ask that truth governs us all. We have to distance ourselves from a misunderstood *viveza criolla*, to stop thinking that whoever is more cunning, or cheats more, or seeks shortcuts, does better. [. . .] We have to prove that our word and our commitments matter. We have to get back to a culture of work, of effort. Absenteeism has increased and the workday has gotten shorter. That is not good" (statements by former president Macri at the celebration of national independence, available as Carlos E. Cué, "Mauricio Macri pide sacrificios y un cambio cultural en la celebración de los 200 años de Argentina," *El País*, July 9, 2016).

9 Wendy Brown, "Neoliberalism's Frankenstein: Authoritarian Freedom in Twenty-First Century 'Democracies,'" *Critical Times*, Vol. 1, No. 1, January 2018, pp. 60–79.

10 In the context of an electoral campaign, the Instagram page of the former president featured a video in which two interlocutors affirm such culpability on the part of Argentines as it concerns the economic crisis that the country faces: https://www.cronista.com/infotechnology/online/El-video-de-Instagram-de-Macri-donde-se-afirma-que-la-culpa-la-tienen-los-argentinos-20190307-0001.html.

11 Even in the case of Brazil, which during Jair Bolsonaro's administration (2019–22) upheld a nationalist position closer to that prevailing in the core countries, this nationalism was inextricably intertwined with gestures of submission to the "great countries of the North." Consider, for instance, Bolsonaro's enthusiastic participation, despite the COVID-19 pandemic, in the July 4 celebrations at the US Embassy in 2020, widely reported in the media. See "Bolsonaro no usa mascarilla en festejo del 4 de Julio," *infobae.com*, July 4, 2000.

12 The "Conquest of the Desert," led by General Julio Argentino Roca, took place between 1879 and 1885. The objective was to expand the Argentinian national territory toward the south and control the lands actually inhabited by indigenous peoples, subjugating them in the process.

13 After 2016, the Central Bank of Argentina began to replace images of national heroes on banknotes with species endemic to the national fauna. The deer, condor, hornero, guanaco, whale, and jaguar came to replace, among others, Eva Perón, San Martín, and Julio Argentino Roca.

14 Walter Benjamin, *The Origin of German Tragic Drama*, trans. John Osborne, Verso, 2003, p. 166.

Chapter 7 Dialectic of the University

1 Adorno in the last fragment of *Minima Moralia*: "The only philosophy which can be responsibly practised in face of despair is the attempt to contemplate all things as they would present themselves from the standpoint of redemption. Knowledge has no light but that shed on the world by redemption: all else is reconstruction, mere technique. Perspectives must be fashioned that displace and estrange the world, reveal it to be, with its rifts and crevices, as indigent and distorted as it will appear one day in the messianic light. [. . .] But it is also the utterly impossible thing, because it presupposes a standpoint removed, even though by a hair's breadth, from the scope of existence, whereas we well know that any possible knowledge must not only be first wrested from what is, if it shall hold good, *but is also marked, for this very reason, by the same distortion and indigence* which it seeks to escape. The more passionately thought denies its conditionality for the sake of the unconditional, the more unconsciously, and so calamitously, it is delivered up to the world" (Theodor W. Adorno, *Minima Moralia: Reflections on a Damaged Life*, trans. E.F.N. Jephcott, Verso, 2005, p. 247, emphasis added).

2 Theodor W. Adorno, "Sociology and Empirical Research," in Theodor W. Adorno et al. (eds.), *The Positivist Dispute in German Sociology*, trans. Glyn Adey and David Frisby, New York: Harper & Row, 1976, p. 69.

3 Measures that gave a new lease on life to Minister of Economy Martínez de Hoz's policies during the last civil–military dictatorship, which ended in 1983.

4 Particularly on the occasion of the campaigns organized by the academic community in 2016 to protest the fact that 500 people had earned their spot as researchers in the Consejo Nacional de Investigaciones Científicas y Técnicas (CONICET, National Council of Scientific and Technical Research) but were not admitted due to budget cuts spearheaded by the government. Through social media campaigns, the public shaming of the targeted researchers sought to impose the idea that their work lacked utility and, even, sense, bordering on the absurd.

5 See, for instance, Willy Thayer's *The Non-Modern Crisis of the Modern University*, trans. De Bret Leraul (Northwestern University Press, 2024 [1996]), Sheila Slaughter and Larry L. Leslie's *Academic*

Capitalism: Politics, Policies, and the Entrepreneurial University (Johns Hopkins University Press, 1999), Eduardo Rinesi's *Filosofía (y) política de la universidad* (IEC–Ediciones UNG, 2015), and Raúl Rodríguez Freire's *La condición intelectual: informe para una academia* (Mimesis, 2018).

6 The technocratic consequences of a cognitive practice that remains unconscious of its social determinations – to which Adorno refers in several of his texts devoted to the critique of positivism in the social sciences – were also intensely emphasized by Louis Althusser in terms of the "human sciences" during the 1970s. His text "Philosophie et sciences humaines" (*Revue de l'enseignement philosophique*, Vol. 10, No. 6, Aug.–Sept. 1963, pp. 161–217) anticipates, in that sense, his argument in *For Marx* (trans. Ben Brewster, Verso, 2006): if the idea of a "detached knowledge" is without a doubt an abstraction from specific social conditions, this idea does not constitute sheer error but rather produces real effects, insofar as it favors a technocratic conception of knowledge by which it is reduced to a mere technical means to solve problems and is oriented toward ends about which it cannot reflect. It is against this technocratic reduction that Althusser positioned as the best possible defense of science – in deep sympathy with Adorno's idea of a social critique of knowledge – the elaboration of a critique of its current state of techniques, which would allow them to become that which they are not yet: true sciences.

7 Rinesi: see note 5 above.

8 Thayer, *The Non-Modern Crisis of the Modern University*.

9 Slaughter and Rhoades, *Academic Capitalism and the New Economy*.

10 As a token of the impact and reach of entrepreneurial ideology in the canonical institutions of Argentine enlightenment, see the following excerpt from an email sent to school parents by the chancellor of the Colegio Nacional de Buenos Aires in August 2017: "I want to tell you about a new initiative we are calling CNBA Emprende [CNBA Entrepreneurship]. This is an initiative started by alumni whose mission is to create a space for students and graduates where they are encouraged to participate *in the spirit and values of entrepreneurship*. There are a growing number of tools and resources to promote *the entrepreneurial spirit as principle of economic activity*, which generally involves support for entrepreneurs across the different stages of their projects, whether with technical resources, financing, mentorship, networking, professional development, etc" (emphases added). One can consult, too, the invitations to the conferences to promote entrepreneurship sent by CONICET to its researchers here: https://noasur.conicet.gov

.ar/conicet-tucuman-dice-presente-en-una-nueva-edicion-del-club-de-emprendedores/, https://www.conicet.gov.ar/emprender-desde-la-ciencia-y-la-tecnologia/, and https://www.conicet.gov.ar/tag/emprendedurismo/. In relation to the University of Buenos Aires, particularly notable was the invitation sent to its professors in 2018 to attend a course called "Ontological Coaching" which was oriented, according to its promoters, to the overcoming of personal limits that lead to failure.

11 Between 2002 and 2010, 12 new national universities – free and public – were created, 80% of whose student population was made up of first-generation students. In 2002, the Universidad Nacional del Noroeste de la Provincia de Buenos Aires was created; the following year, the Universidad Nacional de Chilecito; in 2007, the Universidad Nacional de Río Negro and the Universidad Nacional del Chaco Austral. In 2009, six new universities opened: the Universidad Nacional Arturo Jauretche, the Universidad Nacional de Moreno, the Universidad Nacional de Tierra del Fuego, Antártida e Islas del Atlántico Sur, the Universidad Nacional de Villa Mercedes, the Universidad Nacional del Oeste, and the Universidad Nacional de Avellaneda. Lastly, in 2010, the Universidad Nacional de José C. Paz was created.

12 Value associated with the recognition that higher education is a social right whose existence requires, in turn, the creation of the material conditions so the most disenfranchised sectors can access and remain at university.

13 Pablo Oyarzún, "Las humanidades, lo público y la universidad," in José Joaquín Brunner and Carlos Peña (eds.), *El conflicto de las universidades: entre lo público y lo privado*, Ediciones Universidad Diego Portales, 2011, pp. 111–31.

Chapter 8 Spectrology of the Right

1 This chapter was originally written shortly after then president Mauricio Macri lost the 2019 presidential elections. On December 10, 2019, Alberto Fernández became president as the head of an alliance of different sectors of Peronismo, some of them also Kirchnerist, that had represented the bulk of the opposition to Macrismo between 2015 and 2019.

2 Horacio González, "La mitad de un echarpe o un canto inconcluso," *Fin de Siglo*, No. 3, 1987, quoted in María Pía López, *Yo ya no: Horacio González: el don de la amistad*, Cuarenta Ríos, 2016.

3 *Translator's note:* Elisa Carrió and Patricia Bullrich were prominent members of the right-wing coalition Juntos por el Cambio, whose

candidate for the 2019 presidential elections was the incumbent Mauricio Macri.

4 On this issue, the image that the Macrista politician Cecilia Negro Farrell tweeted of a chimpanzee eating a banana is telling since it condenses the hatred of popular classes that marks, these days, the militants of Cambiemos, and the National Socialist abhorrence of primates – in contradistinction to the nobility they attributed to dogs and horses. See "Una diputada pampeana trató de 'monos' a los votantes del Frente de Todos," *Página 12*, October 30, 2019.

5 On the subject of Michel Foucault, Eduardo Grüner has suggested – to my mind rightly – that unlike what happens with Marx and Marxisms, here we are dealing with an analytic of power that frequently and paradoxically becomes a metaphysics of power by virtue of the indeterminate omnipotence that Foucault attributes to what he calls power. See Eduardo Grüner, *Lo sólido en el aire: el eterno retorno de la crítica marxista*, CLACSO, 2021, p. 167.

6 Silvia Schwarzböck, *Los espantos: estética y postdictadura*, Cuarenta Ríos, 2016.

7 These objections to the idea of a cultural battle are not voiced from the very contemporary gesture of wholesale rejecting any differentiation or sharp distinction – a rejection that, in any event, should be the object less of celebration and more of critical interpretations. Such an *a priori* rejection of all polarization is misleading when it omits the limits – unconscious but also conscious – effectively at play in any powerful thought. In its unlimited pluralism, it seems to forget that the movement of reflection does not consist only in deploying complexities previously hidden *by* polarities, by strict yeses and nos, but simultaneously, insofar as it is situated thought, that movement of reflection is only possible in and for a position-taking where certain objects are excluded: for instance, when one decides to not deal with certain objects, or speak of a certain topic, or refuse (dogmatically in principle) to use certain terms for certain cases.

8 For Althusser, the true critical practice both at the cognitive level and at the political level is the one that produces a break, discontinuity in the self-evidence of the present and dominant ideologies. However, he adds that when a break like that takes place, we ascertain that its temporality is rather more like a process than an instant; that we have been dealing less with the emergence of something absolutely new than with a continuous recommencement, of an incessant fissure that furthermore disappears in the very moment in which it ceases to produce itself as such. There where it existed and continues to exist, the break is unceasing; it takes place in the modality of that which insists and not as a rift with a certain state of things or comprehension all at once. On the subject

of a materialist philosophy, Althusser writes: "it only exists in so far as it occupies a position, and it only occupies this position in so far as it has conquered it in the thick of an already occupied world. It therefore exists in so far as this conflict has made it something distinct, and this distinctive character can only be won and imposed in an indirect way, by a detour involving ceaseless study of other, existing positions" (Louis Althusser, *Essays in Self-Criticism*, trans. Grahame Lock, New Left Books, 1976, pp. 165–6). This break only exists to the extent that the operation of breaking is *continuous* in the exercise of a reading that produces it as insistent (re) commencement, says Natalia Romé in her treatment of this topic in her doctoral dissertation. See Natalia Romé, "La encrucijada materialista: una reconstrucción de la problemática althusseriana en torno a la articulación entre coyuntura y práctica política," Facultad de Ciencias Sociales, Universidad de Buenos Aires, 2014, MIMEO, p. 120.

9 See chapter 7 note 10 above.
10 See chapter 6 note 12 above.
11 Walter Benjamin, "The Author as Producer," in *Understanding Brecht*, trans. Anna Bostock, Verso, 1998, pp. 85–103.

Chapter 9 Chainsaw Capitalism: The Milei Moment

1 This chapter was written in 2025, six years after I finished the previous chapters.
2 Leo Lowenthal and Norbert Guterman, *Prophets of Deceit: A Study of the Techniques of the American Agitator*, Harper and Brothers, 1949, p. 142.
3 See "Palabras del Presidente de la Nación, Javier Milei, en el Encuentro de los Líderes en El Cronista," December 5, 2024, available at: https://www.casarosada.gob.ar/informacion/discursos/50808-palabras-del-presidente-de-la-nacion-javier-milei-en-el-encuentro-de-los-lideres-en-el-cronista.
4 Milei: "We have plenty of energy, plenty of cold, inhospitable land, and plenty of high-quality human resources. It's not for nothing that we're the country with the greatest number of technological unicorns per capita in the region. These three factors combined make up a perfect storm to attract high-quality investors in artificial intelligence." This is an excerpt of a speech by Javier Milei from December 10, 2024, delivered after one year of holding office, available as "Discurso del Presidente Javier Milei en cadena nacional por el año de gestión" here: https://www.casarosada

.gob.ar/informacion/discursos/50817-discurso-del-presidente-javier-milei-en-cadena-nacional-por-el-ano-de-gestion

5 See chapter 3 note 13 above.

6 See the summary provided by the Centro de Estudios Legales y Sociales (CELS, Center for Legal and Social Studies) in their balance sheet on the first year of Milei's administration: "During this year, there was a deepening of the project of social disciplining through the repression of protests and the criminalization of protestors and organizers. Empty streets were celebrated by the government as one of its achievements. At the same time, social organizations were stigmatized, persecuted and criminalized. [. . .] The expansion of state intelligence and surveillance activities accompanied this hardening of the State's repressive apparatus. The rhetoric, reiterated again and again, of terrorism as an internal and external threat has become the main justification for increased social control and the weakening of constitutional guarantees of citizens. Toward the end of the year, the government took one further step in the revindication of the armed forces, linked to this idea of hardening, enabling them by decree to intervene in security tasks when facing non-state external threats and in order to safeguard undefined strategic objectives. So, a symbolic militarism has followed the decision to have a concrete tool ready to hand. In the realm of government decisions, the Executive Office demonstrated its capacity to change the rules of the institutional system through decrees and rulings. With the blank check provided by extraordinary executive powers, it continues to modify the normative infrastructures without much social or political debate" (Paula Litvachky, "Un año en alerta," December 21, 2024, available at: https://www.cels.org.ar/web/opiniones/un-ano-en-alerta/). Moreover, in a report by CELS about social policies, we read: "The definitions expressed by the government in the budget law of 2025 crystallize the undoing and punishment of the policies that uphold life. Today a cluster of seven measures and isolated policies remain, which is insufficient in a scenario that shows grave signs of structural social damage. Over 49 policies related to care have been removed, 24 have been derogated or dismantled, and 18 are in danger. These last have not been allocated resources or have been reduced by design, a situation that is reflected in the poorly executed budgetary function. It has been consolidated as government common sense that paying interest on foreign debt and fiscal balance are more relevant and should limit access to social rights. This translates into damages to people with fewer resources who care for and are cared for" (report available at: https://www.cels.org.ar/web/wp-content/uploads/2024/10/LCD-3.pdf).

7 Max Horkheimer, "The Jews and Europe," in Stephen Eric Bronner and Douglas MacKay Kellner (eds.), *Critical Theory and Society: A Reader*, Routledge, 1989, p. 78.

8 According to Benjamin, his reflections on the concept of history sought "to apprehend an aspect of history that must establish a definitive break between our way of understanding and the vestiges of positivism, which [. . .] profoundly mark even those concepts of History that are closest and most familiar to us" (Walter Benjamin, *Gesammelte Schriften* 1, Suhrkamp, 1991, p. 1225).

9 Wolfgang Streeck, *How Will Capitalism End? Essays on a Failing System*, Verso, 2016, p. 15, original emphasis.

10 Ibid., p. 37.

11 It is worth remembering that in this century, and sticking to the Latin American context, by 2016 there had been attempts at fairly traditional military coups, usually preceded by violent street demonstrations, against Hugo Chávez in Venezuela (2002), Manuel Zelaya in Honduras (2009), Fernando Lugo in Paraguay (2012), as well as Dilma Rousseff's impeachment in Brazil (2016). The military coup against Evo Morales in Bolivia would follow in 2019. And, as this book was going into press in January 2026, Venezuelan president Nicolás Maduro was kidnapped and deposed by the United States.

12 As Milei remarks and insists on in his speeches, from the perspective of the "libertarian" neoliberal doctrine, cooperation is what eventually obtains when each person follows their own interest, inverting the causal relation between conditions for autonomous action and individual liberty that even some strands of liberalism had accepted. See, for instance, Milei's TED talk from 2019: https://www.ted.com/talks/javier_milei_la_estruendosa_superioridad_del_capitalismo. This talk, which synthetizes Milei's position and to which we will return, was replicated with a few modifications in his talk at Davos in 2024, when he was president. See, on this, the article published in *La Nación*, "Milei en Davos," January 17, 2024

13 Slogan with which Horacio Rodríguez Larreta, the then chief of government of Buenos Aires as a member of Macri's party and Patricia Bullrich's opponent in the primaries of Juntos, ended his campaign during the 2023 primary elections. "It's about a choice of life. [. . .] It's about choosing between those who want violence and those of us who want tranquility," Larreta said in one his ads (available at: https://www.clarin.com/politica/nuevo-spot-horacio-rodriguez-larreta-pedir-voto_3_TAle7GQfCo.html?srsltid=AfmBOoqkYx7e4zjGHdN5RSYwx1hCE-McsuVHXS3kOr5f72WaEb7jz0Km).

14 The slogan of Patricia Bullrich, who was the presidential candidate from Macri's party, Juntos.

15 Milei's campaign slogan during 2023. His party was called La Libertad Avanza.

16 A symptom of what I am calling a post-apocalyptic social sensibility could be the fascination that the figure of the zombie has garnered. In this figure, one finds more than a renewal of the fear of a catastrophe to come, as the sinking of the *Titanic* shook the modern trust in progress in the first decades of the 20th century prior to the World Wars. The zombie world does not represent a fearful but manageable collapse, but a scene of complete death in life, in which evil can no longer be reinscribed along the lines of what Laurent Berlant called "cruel optimism" (*Cruel Optimism*, Duke University Press, 2011) because the failure of life goes beyond all dialectic and the perspective of catastrophe produces a terror but also a fascination with an irreversible, unambiguous absolute. According to my working hypothesis, it is through this mixture of fascination and terror produced by a zombie world that contemporary authoritarianisms achieve part of their efficacy, even though, as we will see in the next section, they don't always do this in the same way. See, on the idea of a zombie neoliberalism, Gustavo Robles, "Affective Counterstrategies and Heterotopic Interventions," in *Beyond Molotovs: A Visual Handbook for Anti-Authoritarian Strategies*, transcript, 2024, pp. 172–9. For an interesting problematization of the idea of cruel optimism as culturally dominant, see Wendy Brown, *Nihilistic Times: Thinking with Max Weber*, Harvard University Press, 2023.

17 The term is journalist Baby Etchecopar's, who is referring to public employees and social security recipients during the Kirchner dispensations. See, for example, https://www.youtube.com/watch?v=PnC3Gj1zKzo.

18 *Translator's note: casta*, literally "caste," is Milei's preferred term of abuse for politicians who are his political opponents, whether Peronists or "insiders." Not unlike Trump's "swamp" in the US context.

19 Javier Milei, TED Talk, 2019. See note 12 above.

20 Milei: "I would like to leave a message for all businesspeople here. [. . .] Do not be intimidated by either the political class or parasites who live off the State. [. . .] You are social benefactors, you are heroes. [. . .] Let no one tell you that your ambition is immoral. If you make money, it's because you offer a better product at a better price, thereby contributing to the general wellbeing. [. . .] Long live freedom, goddamnnit!" (conclusion to Milei's speech at the World Economic Forum in 2024, available at: https://www.youtube.com/watch?v=Pfcd0gWNIog).

21 Milei: "Today I'm here to tell you that the Western world is in danger. It is in danger because those of us who are supposed to

defend the values of the West are coopted by a vision of the world that inevitably leads to socialism and therefore poverty. [. . .] The main leaders of the Western world have abandoned the model of freedom for different versions of what we call collectivism" (beginning of Milei's speech at Davos cited in note 20 above).

22 The chaotic, pseudo-plebeian, pseudo-emancipatory tone of Milei's interpellation was well demonstrated in the closing event of his campaign in August 2023. An interminable series of quasi-futuristic images of exploding bombs and demolished buildings followed by an imposing lion set aflame were displayed on gigantic stadium screens, after which Milei emerged accompanied by loud rock music, whose lyrics he himself began to scream. He then said: "Collectivism is a model in which in order to sell, work, eat, or study we have to get a bureaucrat's permission. Some madness they've thrown us into! [. . .] Today we have the opportunity to embrace ideas of freedom and break with the current state model, which only benefits the people who live off the State. [. . .] I'm not asking for your vote so I get power; I'm asking for your vote in order to return to you freedom, so you can once again be the architects of your own destiny. Don't stay at home. [. . .] Long live freedom, goddamnit!" (excerpt from Milei's speech at the end of the first round of elections in 2023, available at: https://www.youtube.com/live/PQ4g77t8oqQ?si=yf4PN_vgxJPKNGt-&t=768).

23 According to Ernst Bloch, one of the major theorists of utopia in the 20th century, there could be utopias of various political valences, but they always relate to emotions he calls "expectant" (such as fear, terror, hope, and confidence) as opposed to those he calls "filled" (envy, greed, and admiration). While the latter emotions "are those whose drive-object lies ready, if not in respective individual attainability, then in the already available world," expectant emotions, by contrast, are those "whose drive-object does not yet lie ready. [. . .] All emotions refer to the actually temporal aspect in time, i.e. to the mode of the future, but whereas the filled emotions only have an unreal future, i.e. one in which objectively nothing new happens, the expectant emotions essentially imply a real future; in fact that of the Not-Yet, of what has objectively not yet been there" (Ernst Bloch, *The Principle of Hope*, Vol. 1, trans. Neville Plaice, Stephen Plaice, and Paul Knight, MIT Press, 1986, pp. 74–5).

24 See Eduardo Grüner, *The Haitian Revolution: Capitalism, Slavery, and Counter-Modernity*, Polity, 2020.

25 Horacio González, "Humanismo y terror," in María Pía López and Guillermo Korn (eds.), *La palabra encarnada: ensayo, política y nación. Textos reunidos de Horacio González 1985–2019*, CLACSO, 2021, pp. 757–62.

26 *Translator's note: el campo* is shorthand for economic sectors involved in the agriculture and livestock industry and the exportation of raw materials.
27 Excerpt from Milei's closing speech at the end of the first electoral round in 2023 (see note 22 above).
28 In these instances, at least half of his time is spent enumerating profoundly surprising statistical "facts," as witness his attempts in the TED Talk already cited (see note 12) to measure "the evolution of gross domestic product from the beginnings of the history of humanity," assuming, of course, that such "measurements" can be made and are available for the year 0.
29 For Adorno's analysis of the techniques of manipulation employed by 20th-century right-wing movements, see, among other works, "Freudian Theory and the Pattern of Fascist Propaganda" (1951), in Andrew Arato and Eike Gebhardt (eds.), *The Essential Frankfurt School Reader*, Urizen Books, 1978, pp. 118–37; "The Meaning of Working Through the Past" (1959), in *Critical Models: Interventions and Catchwords*, trans. Henry W. Pickford, Columbia University Press, 1998, pp. 89–104; and *Aspects of the New Right-Wing Extremism* (1967), Polity, 2020.
30 Lowenthal and Guterman, *Prophets of Deceit*, p. 9.
31 Chile (1973–90): the coup d'état led by Augusto Pinochet, whose government implemented the most radical free market policies in the region, at the behest of the so-called Chicago Boys. Argentina (1976–83): the civil–military dictatorship, which called itself the Process of National Reorganization, also implemented neoliberal policies by then minister of economy José Alfredo Martínez de Hoz. Uruguay (1973–85) and Brazil (1964–85) were also regimes that *de facto* implemented economic models of a neoliberal slant, albeit with some variations and less radically than in Chile and Argentina.
32 William Davies, "The New Neoliberalism," *New Left Review*, 101, Sept./Oct. 2016, pp. 121–34.
33 Cecilia Abdo Férez, *Libertad y cuerpo: escapes de la libertad autoritaria del presente*, Editorial Miño y Dávila, 2025, p. 158
34 Theodor W. Adorno, *Aspects of the New Right-Wing Extremism*, trans. Wieland Hoban, Polity, 2020, p. 7.
35 Ibid., p. 16.
36 Adorno, "The Meaning of Working Through the Past," p. 98.
37 T.W. Adorno, Else Frenkel-Brunswik, Daniel J. Levinson, and R. Nevitt Sanford, *The Authoritarian Personality*, Science Editions, 1964.
38 See chapter 2 of this book.
39 As I have argued elsewhere, support for Milei does not exist *in spite of* the crisis, but *because* of it, and insofar as his government's

policies fulfill his promise to produce the crisis, generalizing what we called above the state of social shelterlessness. See Gisela Catanzaro and María Stegmayer, "Neoliberalismo y sacrificio: entre la moralización y la motosierra," *Orillera: Revista cultural de la Universidad Nacional de Avellaneda* (Undav), No. 8, Fall 2024, pp. 35–44.

40 A recurrent preoccupation of Milei's, which he again brought up in the candidates' debate. See, for instance, "Javier Milei insiste con la compra-venta de órganos," *Página 12*, May 3, 2023, and "Qué dijo Milei sobre el 'el mercado de órganos,'" *La Nación*, November 12, 2023.

41 In Spanish, "Milei" and "*mi ley*" (my law) are phonetically indistinguishable.

42 Lowenthal and Guterman, *Prophets of Deceit*, p. 122.

43 Theodor W. Adorno, *Aesthetic Theory*, eds. Gretel Adorno and Rolf Tiedemann, trans. Robert Hullot-Kentor, Bloomsbury Academic, 2013.

44 Walter Benjamin, "What is Epic Theater?," in *Illuminations*, ed. Hannah Arendt, trans. Harry Zohn, Schocken Books, 2007, pp. 147–54; Walter Benjamin, "Surrealism: The Last Snapshot of the European Intelligentsia," in *One-Way Street and Other Writings*, trans. Edmund Jephcott and Kingsley Shorter, New Left Books, 1979, pp. 225–39.

45 These are struggles that Macri called expressions of a pathologically vengeful spirit. In the terms of a former cabinet member of Macri's government, this time discussing the fact that the government decided to substitute historical figures for animals on banknotes: "The obsession that we have [in Argentina] with analyzing the current conjuncture in terms of the past is not normal. In other countries this doesn't happen. And it's good to know that this is a pathology of ours. For me, one of the two nicest small but symbolic things that we did was to put animals on banknotes. It's the first time in Argentina's history that there are living things on our national currency, and that we leave the dead behind. Leave death in peace; let it rest in peace and let us live our lives" (interview with Marcos Peña from 2017, available at: https://www.youtube.com/watch?v=yO1UX57nfWY).